KNOW YOUR CAR

JOHN DYSON

**Illustrated by
Peter Gregory**

**TVTimes
FAMILY BOOKS**

INDEPENDENT TELEVISION BOOKS LTD, LONDON

INDEPENDENT TELEVISION BOOKS LTD, LONDON
247 Tottenham Court Road,
London W1P 0AU

© John Dyson 1975

ISBN 0 900 72728 4

Printed in Great Britain by
Butler and Tanner Ltd
Frome and London

Also available in this series:

BEATING THE COST OF COOKING
Mary Berry
DEAR KATIE
Katie Boyle
HOUSE PLANTS MADE EASY
Jean Taylor
CARAVANNING
Barry Williams
KNOW YOUR RIGHTS
Dr Michael Winstanley and
Ruth Dunkley
POWER TOOLS AT HOME
Harold King

ACKNOWLEDGEMENTS

Among the many authoritative publications which the author consulted in support of his own knowledge of motoring, particular acknowledgement is due to *Drive* magazine, and to the *AA Book of the Car* (published by Drive Publications Limited). Also consulted were *Know about Emergency Repairs*, *Know about Servicing your Car*, *Know about Corrosion*, *Know about Car Electrics*, *Know about your Tyres* (all published by the Automobile Association). The author would also like to thank the Ford Motor Company Limited for invaluable assistance.

FOREWORD

Know your Car will help you make sense of the complexities of modern cars and to get better value from motoring. It describes how an ordinary motorist can keep his car in safe and efficient running order without resorting to evening classes.

The book is in no sense as comprehensive as a workshop manual. A clear line is drawn between jobs that the amateur mechanic can hope to do for himself, and jobs that are better left to the professionals.

As it is impossible to cover the many variations of makes and models of cars, use this book only in conjunction with your car handbook.

CONTENTS

PART I
OWNING A CAR

Accidents *will* happen, no matter how well cars are designed or driven. Avoiding accidents is the driver's main concern while on the road, but every driver has bad experiences. If the unfortunate does happen how can you best protect yourself? The means is already there, fitted by law to every new car. All you have to do is make the effort to use it.

THE CLUNK–CLICK TRICK

If you think you can fend off a ton or more with your bare hands with only a split second's warning, then don't bother to wear a seatbelt. To get an idea of the forces involved when a car crashes into a solid object, or hits another car head-on, multiply the weight of your own body by the speed of the car.

If you weigh 10 stone (140 lb) this becomes an effective weight in a 10 mph collision of 1400 lb, or nearly three-quarters of a ton. In a 20 mph crash it doubles to nearly a ton and a half. In a 30 mph collision without a seatbelt you hit the dashboard or windscreen with the same force as you would hit the pavement in a face-down fall from a two-storey balcony.

The arguments for wearing seatbelts are irrefutable, while most arguments against seatbelts are irrational fears or old wives' tales. Many people are afraid to use seatbelts because they worry about being trapped by fire. But only one accident in a hundred involves fire. And if you don't wear a belt the odds are that you would be much too badly hurt to move in any case.

To be effective in an accident a seatbelt must not only be worn, it must be worn *properly*. Most people complain because the diagonal belt is uncomfortable or seems to be wrongly positioned. Serious injuries to the neck caused by seatbelts are practically unknown. It is the horizontal part of the belt, which crosses the lap, that is the critical one.

The lap strap must be positioned comfortably tight across the iliac crests – the bony lumps that jut out in the front of the hips. If the belt rides above these bones there is nothing firm to stop the body flying forwards until the belt is brought up short by the backbone: in an accident this will cause injury by displacing soft internal organs.

As well as keeping the lap strap as low over the thighs as possible, it is essential that the buckle of the seatbelt is positioned at the side of the body and not in front of it. In newer cars this buckle is either fixed, or on the end of a flexible stalk, and cannot be adjusted, but it is still important to keep the lap belt low over the bony parts of the hips.

Retractable seatbelts roll themselves away after use and lock only in an emergency stop. They are more convenient to use because the wearer can lean forward when necessary. Women tend to find them uncomfortable because the constant pressure of the rewind spring keeps the belt too tight across the chest. On long journeys this can be eased by clipping an ordinary clothes-peg to the belt where it passes through the slide on the door pillar. It will not interfere with the performance of the belt in an accident, but must be removed before the belt will retract itself.

SEATBELT CHECKS

△ Ensure there are no twists in the belts.
△ Make sure the belt is not snagged on the under part of the seat.
△ Tension in the belt should be just sufficient to allow the flat of the hand to pass between the diagonal strap and the chest.
△ Lap section of the belt must be low over the bony parts of the hips.
△ Buckle of the belt must be at the side of the body, never in front.
△ Make a habit of hanging up the belt immediately after use so it does not become dirty or tangled.

PROTECTING CHILDREN

A child should never be allowed to travel in the front seat – on cushions, using an adult seatbelt or, worst of all, on the knees of a front-seat passenger. In an accident the child on the front seat is ideally placed to hurtle straight through the windscreen or into the dashboard. No adult has a hope of keeping hold of it.

Children should always travel in the back as a matter of routine, even when the front seat is empty, and should sit down. Most cars have special latches which, when set (see your car handbook), prevent the near doors from being opened from the inside. The ideal safety device is an approved child seat or harness. These are made especially for the job and can be fitted, with a little effort by a home handyman, or by a garage, to most cars.

Many so-called car seats for children are positively dangerous and also illegal, so it is essential to check that the seat has been built to the British Standards Institution's specifications and that it carries the Kitemark. The straps bolt to the frame of the car and do not fix to the seat, which in most cars is held only by a couple of small screws. In some systems, the same fittings can be used for carry-cot restraint, child seat and child harness. When a baby is too small for a child seat, it should travel in a carry-cot with its head nearest the centre of the car where it will be safer if the car is hit from the side.

Approved safety seats are designed for children weighing from 20 to 40 lb; they should then graduate to a harness, which will be suitable up to 80 lb. In practice, this means that a child should use a seat from the time he can comfortably sit up until he outgrows it. When using a harness it is important to ensure that the lap part of the belt is tightly adjusted over the bony parts of the hips and is not permitted to ride up over the soft parts of the tummy. The child should not sit on cushions.

If a child's head tends to loll forward when he is strapped in a seat, a cushion can be stuffed behind the lower part of the seat to tilt it just enough to prevent this happening, allowing the child to sleep more comfortably.

SAFE AGAINST WHIPLASH

Many drivers fit accessory headrests to their cars for one or both of two reasons — for comfort, especially for the front-seat passenger who can doze off on long trips; for safety in the event of a rear-end collision. 'Whiplash', caused when the head is bent too far backwards too quickly, as happens when a car is hit from behind, may not be apparent for several days, but the effects can last for months and are unpleasant.

When a headrest is fitted only for safety it must be adjusted properly, as tests have shown that a badly adjusted headrest could add to injury. The strong frame of the head-pad, which you can locate by squeezing the foam covering, must be level with the line of the eyes. If it is lower, there is a danger that the head can be bent even more sharply backwards than it would be without a headrest.

Headrests built into the seat itself by the car manufacturer, such as those in Saab and Peugeot cars, are built to safety specifications and should prevent the head tilting back more than 45 degrees, well within the safety tolerances for most people. However, the fitted headrests, too, must always be properly adjusted.

According to rigorous simulated crash tests carried out by the AA, the best type of accessory headrest is the one-piece type. Adjustable headrests tend to fail because the wire frame bends or the adjusting knobs give way, but this type may be quite adequate for comfort purposes as long as it is positioned high enough.

HEADREST CHECK

△ Ensure the strong part of the head-pad is level with the line of the eyes.

△ Check that there are no sharp edges on the headrest which could endanger rear-seat passengers in a front-end collision.

SEATBELTS
Side view showing correct adjustment.

HEADREST
One-piece type showing internal frame level with line of the user's eyes.

Adjustable type showing internal frame of head-pad level with user's eyes.

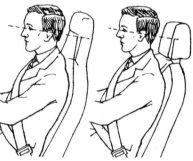

CHILD SEATS
Approved seat (KL Jeenay, Britax, Mothercare) with cushion crammed behind lower part to tilt it just enough to prevent child's head lolling forward.

5

The art of all driving is anticipation. Think ahead: work out what is going to happen so it can be avoided smoothly and in good time. When driving too fast every driver knows the feeling of how all the senses become alert for signs of danger. But the driver should always be alert, because accidents happen when they are least expected. The driver should develop a sixth sense for signs – on and off the road – which could spell trouble.

READING THE ROAD

IN TOWN

1 Give a battered car a wide berth, it betrays a thoughtless and careless driver: another bump may mean little to him but trouble for you.
2 When following an empty taxi look ahead on both sides of the road for a pedestrian who may suddenly hail from the kerb: the taxi is likely to swerve, stop dead in the middle of the road or give unfamiliar signals.
3 Watch for cars with foreign number-plates, left-hand drive, and 'Visitor to Britain' window stickers: drivers likely to be uncertain, or thrusting.
4 Unwritten rules of city driving are that taxi gives way to taxi, bus to bus and even certain cars (such as VW Beetles) let each other through: watch for sudden stops or unexpected behaviour.
5 A long vehicle in the right-hand lane at a roundabout or intersection may be turning left: can you see its indicator? Think twice before going inside it.
6 When a pedestrian, crossing an intersecting road ahead, suddenly steps back on the kerb there is obviously a hidden car coming out: will it stop for you?

IN THE COUNTRY

1 Skid marks on the approaches to a bend show that other drivers have had to brake sharply: clearly the bend is sharper than it looks; slow down.

2 Fresh cow pats on the road, new hedge clippings or grass cuttings, mud from tractor wheels: all show the alert driver there could be obstacles ahead.

3 At night treat with respect any vehicle with a single headlight: it might be a motor-cycle, it might be a wide car with only its nearside headlight working.

4 Lorries with muddy wheels or carrying rubble could well have lumps of clay or broken bricks wedged in their rear wheels which are liable to fly out: hang well back.

5 Be courteous to horse vans and horse boxes: if you overtake, then have to pull in front and brake sharply, the other vehicle will also have to stop suddenly, endangering the lives of the horses it is carrying.

6 In cold weather approach slowly any heavily shaded bit of road such as cuttings, hollows, woods or small bridges (which tend to be in valleys): danger of ice.

If two things can be counted on to bring drivers out in a cold sweat they are fog and skids. And in very cold weather, when fog freezes into black ice on the road, you might be unlucky enough to strike both simultaneously.

MAKING SENSE OF A MOTORING NIGHTMARE

FOG

The first rule of driving in fog is avoid it at all costs. Leave the car in a safe place if you can and take a train, cancel any appointments, knock up friends in the middle of the night and beg a night's sleep on their sofa, but don't drive in fog if it can possibly be avoided. Fog is probably the worst road hazard of all because it leaves drivers nearly blind.

On the other hand, it's easy enough to be caught out in fog unexpectedly with no refuge at hand. Then you have to make the best of it, but it needn't be frightening if you drive slowly and carefully, always within the limits of the visibility. If a stationary object looms up ahead can you stop before hitting it? If not, you are going too fast and you have only yourself to blame.

In fog it is easy to lose all sense of proportion. There is nothing by which to gauge speed. It is important to make continual checks on the speedometer so speed doesn't creep up unnoticed.

Slow, confident progress is preferable to erratic bursts and uncertain steering which do nothing for the nerves at a time when you need to be cool, relaxed and self-assured. Ignore any drivers behind, they are probably pleased to follow the leader. If somebody clearly wants to get by let him do so, but avoid the temptation to keep up with him.

Use dipped headlights, or foglights, but never rely only on sidelights. This is particularly important in misty conditions when traffic still travels fast. Sidelights only are inadequate, and you can soon tell by watching cars coming the other way — in misty weather you see the cars before you see their sidelights. Remember, lights cost nothing to run.

When slowing down, touch the brake pedal lightly to illuminate the brake lights which will warn the car behind; flashing hazard lights are also a useful warning to drivers behind that you are slowing down or stopping in an emergency.

If following another vehicle remember that it will be parting an avenue through the fog so that conditions will seem much clearer than perhaps they really are. Think most carefully before pulling out to overtake the first

of a convoy of cars, and make sure that you can see all the roadway you need. In very thick fog sound is often a help: open the side window and turn off the radio.

Keep the windscreen clean as globules of moisture can make the fog look thicker than it is, and don't screw up your eyes or gaze at the end of the bonnet because then you will begin seeing things that are not there. Exercise the eyes regularly by transferring the focus to the speedometer and rear-view mirror.

Patchy fog is particularly dangerous, especially on main roads and motorways at night. Resist the impulse to increase speed between patches. If you break down or have to stop get right off the road immediately. On motorways it is safer to pull of the hard shoulder on to grass, but if the car has to remain on the hard shoulder get out quickly and sit on the bank well out of harm's way, as many motorway accidents occur on hard shoulders.

FOG CHECK

△ Slow right down and drive evenly.
△ Stay within the limits of the visibility.
△ Use dipped headlights, or foglights, even in mist.
△ Keep the windscreen clean.
△ Never overtake; follow another vehicle if you can.
△ Relax.
△ Get off the road as soon as possible.

FOGLIGHTS

The nearside foglight throws a long narrow beam to illuminate obstructions near the kerb, the other should cast a low apron of light over the road; there is little advantage in using yellow lights.

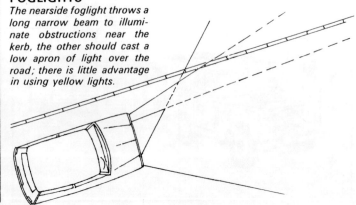

SKIDDING

Skidding is a year-round problem because it can happen on any wet road, let alone one that is icy or oily. It is most likely to occur when braking, or when taking a bend too fast, and it happens very swiftly. In ordinary motoring a skid is always a mistake, and should be rectified at once. Skidding is much less nightmarish if you practise on a skid-pan and learn the correct responses. Some driving schools and some local authorities make skid-pans and expert instruction available to ordinary motorists.

HOW TO AVOID SKIDS

△ *Keep tyres in good condition, at correct pressure.*
△ *Roads are especially slippery when first wetted after a long dry period: slow down.*
△ *Avoid braking, slow down by using the gears.*
△ *Slow down on the straights before bends, change down a gear, then accelerate gently while driving round the bend.*
△ *Look ahead to avoid sudden stops, drive smoothly.*

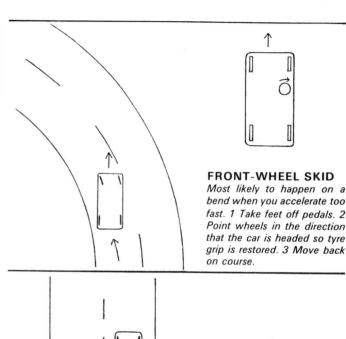

FRONT-WHEEL SKID

Most likely to happen on a bend when you accelerate too fast. 1 Take feet off pedals. 2 Point wheels in the direction that the car is headed so tyre grip is restored. 3 Move back on course.

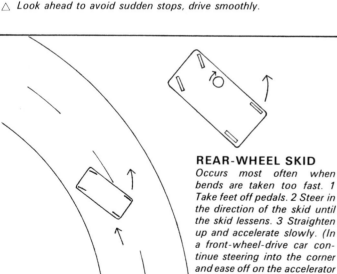

REAR-WHEEL SKID

Occurs most often when bends are taken too fast. 1 Take feet off pedals. 2 Steer in the direction of the skid until the skid lessens. 3 Straighten up and accelerate slowly. (In a front-wheel-drive car continue steering into the corner and ease off on the accelerator until the car comes into line.)

FOUR-WHEEL SKID

Usually the result of sudden fierce braking on a wet road: the whole car slides swiftly ahead, out of control, losing little speed. Release the brakes to restore grip then pump them firmly and smoothly but do not let the wheels lock; if necessary steer round the obstacle ahead.

When you travel as passenger in a car the driver is a very special person. He has your life in his hands. It's no time to start an argument or to persist in little mannerisms that set his teeth on edge. His irritation will show in his driving and affect his judgement so he is more likely to take risks. There is a positive art to being a good car passenger which can contribute to road safety.

THE ART OF BACK-SEAT DRIVING

A good driver is a relaxed driver whose eyes are kept on the road, senses alert, mind on the job. It is the passenger's job to keep him that way. Few people who ride in the passenger seats realise what a vital role they play in this respect — even mothers-in-law!

The first rule of successful co-driving is don't put the driver's back up. If he becomes tense and irritated his driving is bound to suffer. In other words, if he wants the radio on and the window open, don't argue — a stream of fresh air blowing into his face might be essential to prevent him nodding off.

The second rule is to provide information, not advice. A passenger can frequently see blockages ahead that cannot be seen by the driver. It is better to tell him that there is a van parked ahead than to suggest that he moves into the outside lane, because that leaves his options open and he doesn't feel hurried.

And the third rule is to be at his beck and call. The front-seat passenger should be something between a nursemaid and a waiter. If he wants a sweet find it for him. When a driver starts fumbling in the glovebox accidents are likely to happen.

If he must smoke while driving, light his cigarette for him, at night giving him warning so he is not startled by the flame, and shield the light as much as possible from his eyes. Pass the cigarette (cold end first) by holding it against the lower edge of the windscreen in the vicinity of his left hand, so his eyes do not have to stray far from the road to see it. Biscuits, chocolates and sweets (unwrapped) should also be passed in this way.

If you see a sudden emergency . . .

DO warn the driver in an audible and clear voice by describing exactly what is happening up front. For example, say, 'There's a dog under that parked car ahead!' or, 'That child coming out of the sweet shop is running into the road!'

DON'T stamp your feet suddenly on the floor, jerk your body, point suddenly or scream, because he won't know what it is he should be avoiding and in any case, being more alert, may already have seen the hazard. Behaving jumpily in this way affects the driver considerably and his driving will become twitchy.

When the driver asks, 'Is it clear on your side?' . . .

DO give a positive answer in a clear and loud voice, such as 'All clear' if there are no cars coming, or 'Stop' if he should not pull out. Give warning of gaps coming up, such as 'All clear after the dark green Cortina'.

DON'T be vague, mumble or merely answer 'No', because that could mean anything; don't say, 'All clear after the next one', because he may not know which the next one is.

When waiting at a junction to turn on to a main road . . .

DO sit still so the driver can either lean forward to see in front of you or lean back to see behind you.

DON'T move your head back and forth, or turn it from side to side, because this will interfere with the driver's clear vision; don't give the driver advice unless he asks for it.

When reading a map . . .

DO learn to read it well, so you don't make mistakes. If necessary discuss the route with him before you start the journey, or when you stop. Give directions well in advance, especially on motorways, so the driver can move into the nearside lane ready to take the slip road in plenty of time. Give instructions clearly and in a steady voice: 'In half a mile we have to make a right turn on to the A40, probably signposted Oxford or Bristol . . .'

DON'T point when you are telling him which way to go, because your sudden motion can be startling and in any case he will have to turn his head to see which way you are pointing. Don't be afraid of telling him if you are confused, then he can stop in a layby and help you sort it out. It will help him if you are honest: 'We have to take a small side road to the left shortly but I don't know if it's signposted . . .'

When driving a long distance and feeling tired . . .

DO listen to the radio station of the driver's choice, encourage him to wind the window down if he wants and adjust the heating and ventilation to suit himself; fall in with his plans to stop when he feels it's necessary, but if he wants to press on don't argue.

DON'T insist on a hot and stuffy car that will keep you warm and cosy and send you to sleep — it might send him to sleep as well.

When travelling through the countryside . . .

DO explain things that you wish to draw his attention to, and tell him where to look, so he can take his eyes off the road in his own good time, and when it is safe to do so.

DON'T shout 'Look at that!' and point, because he might think you are indicating some emergency: he could brake or swerve violently, and his nerves will become rattled.

Travelling with children

Rules for children in cars should be strict and simple: Sit down. Don't play with the door handles. Talk quietly. Don't kick or touch the driver's seat. You must instil into them a respect for the driver, who should never have to turn round or be involved in any way with looking after the children in the back seat while he is driving.

In this way the adult passengers can be of enormous assistance to the driver: they should appoint themselves chief child-watchers. If the driver must keep an eye on the children, a slip-on wide-angle mirror, obtainable from any motor accessory shop, will give a view of the interior of the car as well as of the road behind. A small rear-view mirror mounted on a rubber suction pad and used by the front-seat passenger to watch children in the back will save constant turning around.

DO encourage children to play games in the car, such as observation contests (counting gates, looking for letters of the alphabet in sequence, etc).

DON'T let children read, play with pencils or scissors, or give them puzzles or books, because the concentration is likely to make small children sick.

DO make regular stops and give children time to run around and stretch their legs.

DON'T give optimistic arrival times or say 'We'll be there soon'. The journey will seem to the children to last forever.

DO travel in the back seat with the children if it's necessary to comfort them.

DON'T under any circumstances allow children to sit on your knees in the front or put them in the same safety belt as yourself.

DO put children in safety seats (and later in harnesses) from an early age so the clunk—click trick becomes habit.

DON'T allow children to stand on the back seat, lean out of the window or put their heads out of a sunshine roof.

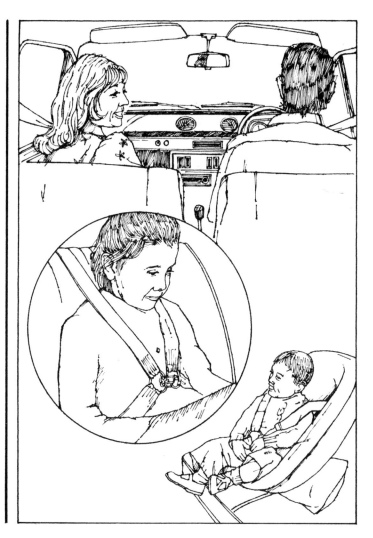

Scope for leisure activities is enormously increased when the car is equipped for towing. Touring with a caravan is an exciting and self-contained way of exploring new places and foreign countries; a sailing dinghy or water-ski boat can be trailed behind a small family car; an ordinary trailer is useful when camping, for do-it-yourself jobs and for carrying other sports equipment such as diving gear or even a dismantled glider.

DRIVING WITH A TRAILER

The main rule when choosing a trailer is to ensure that the loaded weight of the trailer does not exceed the unladen weight of the car. When calculating this take into account all the equipment that goes into the trailer. A caravan may contain food, water, bedding and clothes. A motor-boat might also have its outboard, petrol, anchor and water-skis to be considered.

It is also important to make a sensible match between the cubic capacity of the car and the weight being towed. A six-cylinder engine will cope with towing much more easily than a four-cylinder engine, but the weights of the cars they are in may not be very different. Garages and motoring organisations can give advice about particular cars.

A car is a willing enough workhorse, but it must be in good condition. Clutch and brakes, in particular, need to be in tip-top order.

Whatever type of trailer it is — caravan, horse-box, boat-trailer — the load should be distributed so the trailer is almost balanced, with a bias towards the drawbar. A man should be able to lift the drawbar of the trailer on to the towing bracket of the car with relative ease. If the weight of the trailer is much heavier than he can manage there will be too much weight on the rear of the car. This will be hard on the rear suspension and will lift the weight off the front wheels to such an extent that the steering will tend to 'float'. Luggage stowed in the boot of the car and adult passengers in the rear seat will make the problem even worse.

If the drawbar is too light, or tends to lift up without assistance, the rear wheels of the car will tend to lose their grip, particularly when the trailer bounces over a bump on a bend. A 'jack-knife' or a nasty skid could result.

Balance can be altered by quite small adjustments to the contents of the trailer, because the front and rear of the trailer overhang its pivot point by such a long way. In a caravan, moving a suitcase from the front to the rear could make all the difference. In a boat-trailer a tin of petrol moved from one end to the other could have a similar effect, and of course the positioning of an object as heavy as an outboard motor could be critical.

EQUIPPING THE CAR

Towing bracket
The weight of the trailer must be taken by a special steel arm bolted to the rigid body of the car. This is called the towing bracket. It is important to select one that is designed to fit your particular car. It can be fitted by a garage, or bought in kit form and fitted by the owner. It will be necessary to take off the rear bumper and you will need to use an electric drill.

Mirrors
A clear view behind, not only of the road but of the trailer itself, is important. Most caravans have windows placed so the driver gets a straight-through view, but when towed by some cars the view is restricted. It is important to pin back the curtains so the view is not obscured.

Various mirror devices can be fitted to the car to assist rear vision: a wide-angle wing mirror, which fits over the existing wing mirror; a long-arm side mirror which juts out from the side of the car to give a clear view but can be dismantled when not in use; a periscope which fits to the roof of the car above the windscreen, using rubber suction cups, and gives the driver a suitable view.

Lights
Kits can be obtained of the wiring required to work the tail lights, brake lights and indicator lights at the rear of the trailer. This is fitted to the car and led back to a seven-pin socket fixed to the towing bracket. The trailer is also wired, and when hitched up to the car the plug on the trailer is simply plugged into the car socket. If it is a boat-trailer, the lights, reflectors, number plate and indicators can be mounted on a detachable board. When the boat is being launched or the trailer is not in use, the board is removed from the stern of the boat with the wiring coiled up, and placed in the boot of the car.

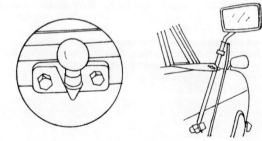

WHAT THE LAW REQUIRES

A car trailer must be no wider than 7 ft 6 in and no longer than 23 ft (if the trailer has four wheels and the towing car weighs at least three tons unladen it can be as long as 39 ft).

The trailer must have:

Brakes on all wheels if, unladen, it weighs more than 2 cwt. The brake can be of the over-run type, but if this type is fitted there must also be a parking brake.

Wings on the wheels (conventional boxed-in caravan-type wings are also permitted).

Number plate, lit up at night, matching that of the car.

Indicators of the flashing amber type.

Two red tail lights.

Two red reflectors, triangular in shape.

Two red stop lights, which work in conjunction with the car's brake lights, if the trailer was made after 1 January 1971. Trailers made before this date must have at least one red stop light.

White sidelights at the front, within 12 in of the outermost point, if the trailer or part of the load extends more than 12 in beyond the outermost point of the car's own front sidelights.

SPEED LIMITS

The normal speed of a car towing a trailer or caravan is 40 mph, but it can travel at up to 50 mph if a roundel bearing the number 50 in black on a white background is stuck on the rear of the trailer or caravan. This may be done only if a) the kerbside weight of the car appears in an easy-to-read position; b) the maximum gross weight of the trailer or caravan is marked on the rear offside; and c) the gross weight of the trailer or caravan does not exceed the kerbside weight of the car.

ON THE ROAD

Towing a trailer is little different from any other driving except that the combination is a great deal more unwieldy than a single vehicle. Take things slower, slow down earlier, avoid sudden stops, do not accelerate too hard, treat the car firmly but gently.

Consideration of other road-users is important. How often have you cursed when stuck behind a caravan? Well, don't give others cause to curse you. When there is a line of vehicles behind pull over to let them by.

In cross-winds and on long straight roads such as motorways the sway of a large trailer is particularly evident. It causes the front of the car to wander from side to side and sometimes this movement, which can be a little frightening, is difficult to check. Experiment with ways of stopping it, by slowing down and by gentle acceleration. If it occurs persistently or makes control of the car difficult, there is something more seriously wrong: check tyre pressures, weight balance and steering.

REVERSING

Reversing a trailer is a little like trying to push three pennies in a straight line along the desk with your finger on only one of them.

It is important to have a helper standing by to guide you, and to ensure that nobody walks behind the trailer as it begins to move. The helper should indicate with hand signals which way the back of the trailer is to move, leaving it to the driver to work out how to steer. He should stand where he can be clearly seen by the driver.

The secret is to carry out every manoeuvre at dead-slow speed, but avoid riding the clutch which will burn out quickly if it slips with such a lot of weight on the car.

Before taking the combination on a main road or into a crowded area, it is wise to practise reversing a few times in and out of your drive to get the hang of it. It is better to make your mistakes at home than in a busy city carpark.

TRAILER CHECKS

△ Are tyres in good order, pressures correct?
△ Do all the rear lights work, have you got spare bulbs?
△ Is the weight evenly distributed on board?
△ Does your motor insurance policy cover trailers?
△ Is the trailer plus contents insured?

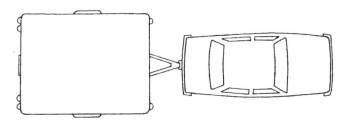

Loading a car is a matter of common sense. But there is a temptation, because the car does not immediately stagger under the strain, to overload. A boot full of heavy suitcases, a roofrack piled high with luggage plus four or five adult passengers is a trial for any car. It won't complain, but it will probably break. And at a most inconvenient moment at that.

PACKING THE CAR

The important things to remember when loading a car are that the load is spread evenly, that the load is not too high so the car's centre of gravity is affected (and is therefore more likely to tip over on a bend) and that the car is not too far down on its springs.

If the car is loaded up and you feel a hard thump as you go over the first small bump be prepared for trouble during the rest of the journey, because this means the car is 'bottoming' on its springs. They simply cannot cope with the load you've put on them.

Most modern cars can carry four passengers and a reasonable amount of personal luggage with ease, but avoid the temptation to put a massive suitcase on the roofrack to make more room in the boot.

A number of smaller soft luggage containers can be packed into a boot more easily, as a rule, than large hard-covered suitcases. Boots and shoes pack conveniently into the small spaces that are left, and raincoats and heavy pullovers can be spread over the top to be immediately to hand should you need them.

Cardboard or plastic boxes without lids, which slide under the front seats from either the front or the rear, like drawers, are useful for extra storage space for maps, pencils and sweets, leaving more room on the parcel shelf and in the glovebox.

Do not put hard-edged or heavy objects on the rear parcel shelf where they can fly forward and hurt somebody in an emergency stop. If there are children in the rear of the car a small box on the seat for their toys is a good idea and, if they are under the age of about six, the space between the front and rear seats can be filled with such things as rugs, carrier bags and other slender items of luggage. Blankets take up less room if they are carried flat on the back seat, with children sitting on them. They can snuggle under them if they get tired.

The law says that drivers must not load their cars in a way that is dangerous to other road-users. For example, fishing rods jutting out of a side window may well constitute a hazard. Also the total weight of the car and how it is balanced are important because they may affect the way the car handles.

Tyre pressures should also be increased when there is a heavy load in the car (see instructions in your car handbook), but remember to decrease the pressure again when the load is removed to restore normal handling.

ROOFRACKS

Although luggage carried on the roof impairs the car's performance, increases fuel consumption and cuts down speed, it is a convenient way of carrying light bulky items.

The roofrack (and the load on it) must be as low as possible and it is important to make regular checks on the bolts fixing the roofrack to the car. After fitting the rack, drive the car for two or three miles before loading it, then check the bolts again.

The roofrack should be packed as evenly as possible. Any material used to cover it must be strong and firmly tied down, as the slipstream will cause it to fray: light polythene lasts only a few minutes before it is torn to ribbons and makes a fearful din. Any zips or fastenings should not face the front or rainwater will force its way in. Loose straps or bits of rope will flutter against the car roof and wear away the paint.

Stretchy rubber luggage grips are ideal for tying down a load on a roofrack, but when fixing them on make sure the hook on the opposite side of the car is firmly in place before stretching the rubber, for it can catapult across the car into your face if it works itself free.

Take every opportunity to check the roofrack and the luggage lashings during the journey. And treat any car in front with a heavily loaded roofrack very warily, for roofracks falling into the paths of cars behind are a common cause of accidents, particularly on motorways.

PACKING THE CAR

1 *Roofrack: lightweight luggage as low as possible.*
2 *Slender items will go behind the front seats if young children are in the rear.*
3 *Children can sit on rugs spread flat on rear seat.*
4 *Small packages are better than large in the boot.*
5 *Put shoes and small objects in the gaps.*
6 *Keep raincoats readily accessible on top.*
7 *Open boxes under the front seats make good drawers.*

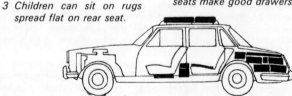

From Britain a motorist has all Europe, North Africa, Asia Minor and Scandinavia within relatively easy driving distance. During the summer there are more than a hundred ferry and hovercraft crossings outward bound every day, so the 'wet bit' of your journey is simple. Although one must drive on the right, motoring in Europe has become increasingly straightforward as more and more road signs and driving rules are standardised.

GOING ABROAD

Driving abroad is a new dimension in motoring, but the problem that worries most people is driving on the right. In fact this is quickly mastered, although it takes a day or two to overcome the initial feeling of strangeness. While driving abroad the difficulty is making the right responses – if a truck comes whistling round the corner will you *remember* to react by steering to the right rather than to the left?

As long as you don't get too worried about it the mind seems to condition itself to do the right thing. Where you may run into trouble is at a roundabout or after emerging from a one-way street. Beware of over-confidence – many drivers have narrow-misses on the last day of their holiday, after hundreds of miles of trouble-free driving throughout Europe.

In general, driving abroad is the same as driving in Britain, but there are still some important differences. In France, for example, you must give way to *everything* coming from the right. Roads in France that have right of way are usually marked by a yellow diamond, and when the priority route ends there is a yellow diamond with a black bar. Many roads entering from the right have stop signs, or give-way signs, but some don't and you can often spot these in advance by looking for skid marks on the surface ahead.

INSURANCE

While it is no longer obligatory to take out extra insurance before going to Common Market countries, it is certainly wise and costs only a small amount. You are given a 'Green Card', which is the international certificate of motor insurance. For some countries, such as Russia, you have to take out special insurance at the border.

It is also wise to take out personal medical and luggage insurance, because in many countries there is no national health system and medical expenses can be exorbitantly high. This can be bought for a modest price at any travel agent or insurance broker.

The motoring organisations offer a first-class motoring insurance which covers you against practically all contingencies. If the car breaks down

irretrievably you can hire a car and your own vehicle will be brought home free of charge by transporter; medical and hotel expenses can also be covered.

The insurance 'package' also transports spare parts out from England free of charge, provides a chauffeur if the driver in the family can no longer drive and offers a flying ambulance service if you are seriously injured or ill far from home. Theft, cancellation, loss of tickets and many other eventualities are also covered, and the policy can be extended to include caravans or other types of trailers.

If going to Spain it is important to have a 'bail bond', which can be obtained from an insurance company to cover the possibility of your car being impounded by police following an accident. Any subsequent fine is taken out of the bail bond, which is returned to the insurance company. You must pay the insurance company the amount of the fine to make up the difference.

DRIVING LICENCE

A valid British driving licence is sufficient for most European countries except Spain. If an international driving licence is required it can be obtained from a motoring organisation. A passport picture and small fee are required. Italy requires a translation of licence details (available from motoring organisations).

GB STICKER

Every British car abroad must carry the letters GB in black on a white background on the rear of the car.

REAR-VIEW MIRROR

To help with driving on the right it is advisable to fit a wide-angle mirror on the interior rear-view mirror so you have all-round vision behind the car. A wing mirror on the car's nearside is also an advantage.

SPARE PARTS KIT

A spare parts kit can be hired from a motoring organisation and includes such things as fan-belt, bulbs, fuses and gaskets. Parts used are charged for on return.

LENS CONVERTERS

Headlights of a British car dip in the wrong direction for continental driving so it is wise to fit lens converters, which are yellow plastic screens that clip over the front of the headlights. Fitting is easily done; make sure they are the right way up. Some headlights can be converted by changing the bulbs or by sticking an opaque film over part of the lenses. The headlights must be reconverted before you start driving again in Britain.

SPEED

Many continental roads are straight, wide and comparatively empty; the motorways in many areas have no speed limit. It is a temptation to keep the accelerator foot hard down. But what often happens is that the car blows up.

Very high speed in hot weather for long periods, especially when the car is heavily laden, can drive a lot of the oil into the upper part of the engine so the lower part is not lubricated: the engine becomes hotter and hotter until it eventually seizes or something breaks.

It is important to vary the speed so the oil has time to drain down into the bottom of the engine at regular intervals: come down to 50 mph for two or three minutes in every ten.

MAINTENANCE

Long spells of very hard driving in hot weather find all the weak points in your car. A radiator hose which has been on the point of going for weeks just can't stand the strain and bursts. Similarly a weak oil seal is subjected to much greater pressure than usual and finally gives way completely. In either case you are left stranded.

Before making a long journey have the car fully serviced and checked for weak points. If anything looks uncertain of lasting a long course of hard driving, fix it or replace it.

Probably the most important decision made in your motoring career is the type of car you will buy. Inevitably it will be a compromise between size, price and performance. Buy a small car handy for nipping round town and easy to park, and you can't expect to travel long distances comfortably. Buy a large car for touring and in town it will feel like a tank. Whatever the car, there are some important points to watch.

BUYING A CAR

The main advantage of buying a new car, apart from the thrill of owning a brand-new object, is reliability. Although there are bound to be one or two teething troubles, particularly if the model of car has not been out for long, these will be fixed by manufacturer's warranty, or guarantee, which lasts normally for twelve months or 12 000 miles, whichever comes first.

However, depreciation of a new car is greatest during its first year, when it can drop in value by as much as 20 per cent. There is a lot to be said for buying a car that is just a year old, with a three-month guarantee offered by a reputable dealer. The worst of the depreciation is over, yet it still has the smell and the feel of a new car.

When buying a car insist on a test drive, but make sure the car is insured. Test engine, road and wind noise. Drive with the windows up and the windows down. Does the car corner well? Are the pedals and the steering light to operate? Are the switches convenient to use? Is visibility good or does the car have awkward blind spots? Is the engine flexible — will the car pull away from 20 mph in top gear or do you have to change down? Is the clutch smooth and light?

If adults ride regularly in the rear seat is there sufficient leg room? Can child safety seats and harnesses be fitted by the dealer before you buy the car?

While driving the car wear the seatbelt and check that it can be positioned correctly, with the lap belt low over the bony parts of the hips and the buckle at the side of the body, not in front. If the seatbelts are of the retractable type do they operate smoothly and firmly?

Light colours, such as yellow and white, should be considered first as they tend to be safer than dark or neutral colours because they show up better in fog or darkness.

Collect as much information as you can about the car. Motoring organisations such as the AA carry out extensive road tests of new cars and their reports are available to members. Motoring magazines also conduct comprehensive road tests which offer a useful means of comparing make with make.

When discussing the price of a new car, remember it is the 'on the road' price that matters – including special car tax, VAT and compulsory extras, such as seatbelts, delivery and number plates.

When buying a car secondhand weigh up how much depreciation is acceptable. Obviously, the older the car the 'looser' it will be. Like buying a middle-aged horse, all you can do is assess how much durability remains in its old bones and how strongly its heart still beats.

When the car has been chosen it is worth paying the small fee involved to have a motoring organisation engineer carry out an independent assessment.

In general, an automatic car can be a good buy because the extra initial cost will have been absorbed in the first year of the car's depreciation; although it will use a little more petrol and there will be some loss of acceleration, the engine will probably have been treated better.

Foreign cars may be good bargains when new, but less good when second hand because spare parts may be in short supply: check this carefully before committing yourself and don't take the salesman's word for it. A motoring organisation such as the AA can answer any queries.

A car that is more than three years old must have a valid DoE Certificate of Roadworthiness (formerly known as the MOT), but this shows only that the car is fit enough to meet the letter of the law, and is by no means a guarantee of trouble-free motoring.

Check the car's logbook to see how many owners it has had, and if necessary contact the last owner, whose address will be listed. It is against the law to misrepresent facts about the history of a car, so it pays to have a witness when you ask the salesman questions such as: Was this a one-driver car? Was it a hire car? Has the car been in an accident?

HOW TO CHECK THE CONDITION OF A SECOND-HAND CAR

BEFORE THE TEST-DRIVE

Rust – look under the doors, under the wings, at joints between wing and bonnet, door sills, headlight reflectors, under carpets.

Collision damage – ripples in the bodywork, a slightly duller or mottled paint indicating that a part has been resprayed, can show that the car has been repaired after a crash.

Suspension – lean heavily on each corner of the car and release it: the car should rise up, then bounce down and up once only.

Tyres – there should be at least 1 mm of tread on each tyre; look closely for damage to sidewalls and for plugs, don't forget the spare.

Water leaks – from the radiator, hoses and other parts of the engine; a greyish stain from anti-freeze is often a tell-tale sign.

Steering – there should be less than $\frac{1}{2}$ in of free play in the steering wheel.

Wheels – jack up the wheels and test for play, which should not exceed $\frac{1}{16}$ in.

Tools – are the jack and wheel-changing equipment complete?

Battery – signs of corrosion can indicate that the battery has recently been leaking acid; are the terminals in good condition?

Hydraulic fluid hoses – they should be strong and in good condition.

Radiator hoses – cracks in the rubber betray their age.

Electrics – are the contacts in good condition, with no twisted or frayed wires?

DURING THE TEST-DRIVE

Clean running – after starting up, step out of the car, have the salesman gun the engine; check that the exhaust smoke is clean and soon disappears.

Lights – walk round the car checking all lights, including headlights on full and dip, indicators, number-plate light, brake lights.

Controls – test them all to make sure they work.

Clutch – does it work smoothly, does it slip?

Brakes – make an emergency stop from about 25 mph (check there is nothing behind you): has the car pulled up smoothly, progressively and in a straight line?

Handbrake – does it hold the car firmly on a hill?

AFTER THE TEST-DRIVE

Oil-leaks – check the engine for signs of new oil (a little seepage is normal) escaping from the engine, but make sure it is not hidden by dirt.

Wheels – remove hubcaps and make sure no oil has been thrown out of the wheel bearings.

Much of the bitterness between motorists and garages stems from ignorance and misunderstanding. Ignorance on the part of the motorist, who doesn't understand how garages operate. Misunderstanding on the part of the garage, whose receptionists speak in technical jargon and fail to make the situation fully clear to laymen. Getting good service from your local garage is essential for trouble-free motoring and your own peace of mind.

MAKING FRIENDS WITH YOUR GARAGE

A garage man is rather like the family doctor. He meets you only when there is something wrong; and you are peeved about it because it's no fun being without your car and having to fork out money to meet large bills.

But the parallel doesn't end there. You don't ask the doctor for a course of penicillin. You tell him your symptoms and let him decide the treatment. The same approach should be made to the garage when something goes wrong with the car.

If you ask for a new gear-box the mechanic will do it, but really the car might need only a clutch reline. You should have told him the clutch was juddering and he would know where to look for trouble – not at the gear-box.

Explain clearly and precisely what is wrong with the car and don't be afraid of sounding foolish. More important, give the mechanic or garage receptionist time to listen – he can't help much if all you want to do is drop the keys and run for a train.

If necessary, ask for a test-drive and demonstrate to the mechanic what the particular fault is, then ask him to drive. This can be a slow job in morning rush-hour traffic, so again allow plenty of time for the garage to be fully briefed. There will probably be other motorists bringing their cars in at the same time.

At large garages servicing is usually done almost on a production-line system by men who have little to do with the workshop, so there is no point in delivering the car to a big garage for a routine service then expecting the garage to carry out a repair job as well.

Also, a garage's workforce is very carefully deployed throughout the day on the basis of the repair jobs which have been booked. Having made a booking several days in advance it is unfair to turn up with an additional list of jobs to be done – although there is no harm in asking.

When considering the cost of a repair job there are three things to take into account:

1 Spare parts, oil, grease, etc.
2 Charge-out rate – the hourly rate for labour.
3 VAT.

It's no good asking only how much a certain part will cost, because the answer may be completely misleading as far as the final charge is concerned. For example, a part may cost only £10 to buy but take four hours to fit at a charge-out rate of £4 an hour – the total bill will be £26 plus VAT and the cost of any smaller parts needed. The motorist could find himself paying three times more than expected.

It is wise to get a written estimate of all the costs of any big job, including labour. If the estimated cost is likely to be exceeded the garage should contact you before continuing with the job. But if it is a fairly routine job, such as relining the brakes, leave your telephone number with the garage so you can be contacted should the mechanic discover a leaking oil seal, for example, which may need repairing at the same time and will incur more expense.

Finding a garage you can trust is important, not because such garages are rare, but because it is unsettling and worrying to feel that important maintenance jobs may have been ignored. Usually it is difficult to check that work has been properly done. The only real proof of an efficient garage is reliability over a long period.

It pays to become a regular customer of one particular garage where your face soon becomes familiar. Buy petrol and all other motoring needs there, open an account if necessary. The garage should be franchised for your make of car, which means that it has been licensed by the manufacturer to stock spare parts, and mechanics will have attended special training courses. It also means that the garage is kept fully up-to-date with any information from the manufacturer on defects which will be put right automatically and free of charge.

When buying a new car it is important to understand the warranty, which usually does not include wear and tear, and adjustments to such things as carburettors, wheel balance, etc. If repairs or servicing are required before a holiday trip, be certain to book in the car in plenty of time, and allow time for any larger jobs to be done should the need arise.

Garages displaying an AA spanner rating, denoting the range of tools, equipment and training, have an agreed code of conduct and complaints by AA members are investigated fully.

Garages which belong to the Motor Agents' Association (MAA) also participate in a complaints procedure which leads ultimately to independent arbitration. If the complaint is justified, in nearly every case a suitable compromise is reached before legal action becomes necessary.

If you feel you have a justifiable complaint, take the matter up first with the garage manager before involving a third party. If you feel it has to be taken further, pay the bill but warn the manager that you will be taking further action. Keep all bills and receipts and contact either a motoring organisation or the MAA as soon as possible.

Insurance is important from two points of view. First, a car represents a substantial investment which insurance protects: if the car is damaged in an accident or stolen, the insurance company will pay for repairs or replacement. Second, a car is a fast-moving object weighing a ton or more which can do a lot of damage to other people and their property: insurance protects others against your mistakes.

KEEPING A GRIP ON THE INSURANCE UMBRELLA

Like an umbrella, insurance is something that motorists carry around at all times but need only when caught out. It is by far the heaviest 'invisible' cost of motoring in the sense that it is paid for in cash once a year and nothing tangible is received in return — apart from a piece of paper which must be shown to a policeman on demand.

Individuals might be prepared to do without insurance, because they think that accidents happen only to other people and that they can afford to risk damage to their own cars.

But few individual motorists could compensate out of their own pockets a person who was badly injured. Accidents happen even to competent drivers, who must often take the blame for accidents that could not have been avoided. There are the victim's medical, legal and repair costs to be considered, as well as loss of earnings and other forms of compensation which have to be made. A motorist without insurance could find himself owing thousands of pounds, which could take a lifetime to repay.

And there are two sides to the matter of compulsory insurance, because it might be you who is the innocent victim: an insurance company will be able to compensate you more readily than will the other driver, who might well be a low-paid worker with his own family to support and no assets.

For obvious reasons, it's risky trying to cut corners when insuring a car. One wrong or deliberately misleading answer on a proposal form, for example, could invalidate the whole policy and you would not discover the fact until a claim was pending. It pays to use a reputable insurance company: unless it is a foreign company it should be a member of the British Insurance Association. There are dangers in using small cut-price insurance companies or brokers. Insurance bargains need to be treated with caution.

Motor insurance is a completely open market so the style and scope of policies vary enormously, even among the familiar, big-name companies. Before taking out an insurance policy, half an hour spent with the Yellow Pages asking for quotations from half a dozen different large insurance companies is time well invested. Each company calculates the premium you pay by weighing up the different risks involved.

1 USE OF CAR

The cheapest insurance is for cars used only for pleasure and domestic purposes, but the premium may be higher if the car is used for commuting to and from work. If the car is used occasionally for business it must be insured for this purpose but the premium is not a great deal higher. If the car carries goods or samples then business is considered to be its main use, and the premium goes up a lot.

2 DRIVER'S OCCUPATION

Each company has a confidential list of occupations which demand a higher premium. Top of the lists are jobs like bookmaker, scrap-metal merchant, anybody in show business and student. Bottom of the lists (paying the smallest premium) are so-called respectable occupations like bank manager, doctor, teacher.

3 NUMBER OF DRIVERS

Premiums are reduced substantially if the number of drivers is limited, preferably to specific people whose names appear on the policy. This means that if the car is driven by somebody else it probably won't be fully insured.

4 ACCIDENT RECORD

Accident-prone drivers pay more than drivers with clean records. Driving-licence endorsements and other penalties for serious driving infringements of the law are also taken into account.

5 WHERE YOU LIVE

A car kept in a garage next to a house in a quiet village will be less at risk than a car kept on the street in a city, so premium scales are correspondingly lower.

6 TYPE OF CAR

The value of the car does not affect the premium as much as its type. A small family saloon with parts that are quickly and cheaply replaced will command a smaller premium than a foreign car for which spare parts are hard and expensive to get. Sports or high-performance cars are judged more likely to be involved in accidents, and some cars – depending on the type of driver – will not get comprehensive insurance at all.

7 PERSONAL QUALITIES OF DRIVER

Premiums are highest for young drivers, particularly teenagers, and lowest for middle-aged drivers with good driving records and established assets such as their own houses and responsible jobs.

It is important that all these facts are accurate when supplied to the insurance company. If the company discovers, in the event of a claim, that you were in fact travelling to a business appointment when the car was insured only for domestic or social use, or that you had failed to supply information of past accidents, the policy could be invalidated.

The main type of insurance, 'comprehensive cover', is the most expensive. It is designed to cover all the expenses that arise from a motor accident, as well as theft of the vehicle, damage by fire, personal possessions in the car and such things as a windscreen broken by a flying stone. After an accident it covers passenger liability, repairs to the car, some medical expenses, some legal expenses and pays a lump sum in the event of death. It also covers claims arising from damage that you do to other cars or property, e.g. a garden wall. If your car is so badly damaged that it is a 'write-off' don't expect a new car – the insurance pays only the current market value of the damaged one.

A cheaper form of insurance is 'third party, fire and theft'. This protects you against claims from other people as a result of injury or damage. The costs of repairs to your own vehicle are not included. But it does cover theft and fire damage to your own car. This type of policy is even cheaper if it is 'third party only'. The saving, when compared with a comprehensive policy, varies. If you have a popular small car the saving is only about one-third, but if it is a big exotic car the saving could be two-thirds.

Finally, there is an insurance policy which covers you to the bare minimum required by the Road Traffic Act. It has many limitations, including the fact that you are covered only when on a public road (the insurance company may not pay up if an accident occurred in a carpark or on a garage forecourt), and is seldom issued. Occasionally it is supplied to drivers who have such a bad record that no company will insure them further.

Insurance premiums can be substantially reduced if you agree to a larger 'excess'. This is the first part of any claim, usually about £15, which the policy-holder must pay. In other words, if you claim for £65 worth of repairs, the insurance company will pay up only £50. An excess of £25 or more can be agreed in which you would receive only £40. Young drivers and people with little driving experience are frequently obliged to accept even larger excesses.

The high cost of motor insurance is reduced by what is known as the 'no claims discount' (NCD) or 'bonus' which rewards the careful driver with a record of safe driving. How an NCD can be earned varies a great deal from company to company.

Some insurance policies are 'short-scale', which means that you achieve maximum discount (approximately 60 per cent) quickly — after four years — but the premium is higher. Typically, a short-scale policy offers a 30 per cent discount after the first year; 40 per cent after the second; 50 per cent after the third; 60 or 65 per cent after the fourth. Other policies are known as 'long-scale', which means that you take longer (six years instead of four) to reach the full 60 per cent discount, and if you do make a claim it can take three or four years instead of two to get back the maximum discount, but the premiums are cheaper.

One anomaly of the system is that a driver who has already earned three or four years' discount will be treated much more harshly in the event of a claim than the driver with only one year's discount, because he has more to lose. When deciding whether to claim, it is important to take into account not only the value of the NCD you lose this year, but next year and the year after that as well. If your NCD is 30 or 40 per cent it is often not worth claiming from the insurance company unless the cost of repairs is greater than the full value of the premium.

It is important to keep the insurance company posted of any changes to the car (new engine, different colour), if you change the car, of any changes of use to which the car is put, or of any new drivers (e.g. children learning to drive).

THE CAR'S PAPERS

INSURANCE CERTIFICATE
Shows that your car is insured sufficiently to meet the requirements of the law and must be produced on demand (or presented at a police station within five days). Must not be as much as one day out of date.

DRIVING LICENCE
Certificate showing that you have passed the official driving test. Must be produced on demand (or presented at a police station within five days). Must be renewed at council offices every three years.

LOGBOOK
This is the car's 'passport', which shows to whom it belongs. Any changes (e.g. colour, new engine, new address) must be officially recorded in the logbook, which should never be kept in the car but in a safe place in the home: if thieves get hold of it with the car they will have no trouble forging change of ownership.

DOE CERTIFICATE OF ROADWORTHINESS
Every car more than three years old must be tested annually by a qualified garage and issued with a Department of Environment Certificate of Roadworthiness (previously known as the MOT test).

ROAD FUND LICENCE
Must be exhibited on the nearside lower corner of the windscreen to show that you have paid the £25 road tax. This can be renewed by post, at certain council offices or at a post office. Insurance certificate, logbook, DoE test certificate (MOT) if applicable and the old licence disc must be supplied with the application. Licences for four-month periods can also be obtained.

Only when the costs of a year's motoring are itemised on paper is it possible to get a real picture of how much the convenience of owning a car is worth. Setting down all costs as they occur helps you to spot where real savings can be made.

THE REAL COST OF YOUR CAR

The cost of motoring is put into perspective when you add everything that has been paid out over a period of twelve months, together with the 'invisible' costs, and work out how many taxi rides and hire cars could have been had for the same price. For the cost of running your own fairly new 1600 cc car for a year, you could take a 50p taxi ride twice on every working day of the year and have enough left over not only to hire a car for a two-week holiday but also for about twelve weekends.

Most people buy their motoring by the gallon – out-of-pocket expenses which can be met fairly easily. Hire purchase or loan repayments are made on their cars by bankers' orders, so the money is never seen changing hands. Other costs, such as parking, are lumped in with household expenses and aren't really considered as part of the costs of running the car.

When it is all added up properly, however, motoring is seen to be the major item of expenditure on most families' budgets – after food, and usually ahead of mortgage payments, house-running costs, clothes and holidays. The cost of motoring must be treated seriously – it's not an incidental expense that can be shrugged off, like the TV licence or weekly magazines.

The surprising fact is that the day-to-day cost of running the car – petrol, oil, servicing, parking – is only about half the total cost. The remainder is absorbed by standing charges which are the same no matter how many miles you drive in a year.

The figures show the ludicrously small overall effect of skimping on such things as servicing, or using a cut-price oil. In the long run both these so-called economy measures save only a tiny amount, but may prove to be a false economy because greater engine wear and more frequent breakdowns result.

The only way to make substantial reductions in the cost of motoring is to reconsider the type of car you drive and the uses to which it is put. Practically all costs are greater for bigger cars, which also depreciate faster than smaller ones and require more capital in the first place.

FUEL CONSUMPTION

Put simply, the difference between a car that does 20 miles per gallon and one that does 40 miles per gallon is that every time you fill it up with petrol you have to pay out twice as much. Most cars do about 10 000 miles a year. The owner of the thirstier 20 mpg car has to buy an additional 250 gallons of petrol every year.

SPARE PARTS

A run-of-the-mill car may not be very splendid if cutting a dash around your neighbourhood is an important part of motoring, but simple ordinary cars are a great deal cheaper to repair than high-performance cars, large cars, or some foreign models.

ABILITY TO HOLD ITS PRICE

Some cars hold their value better than others because they are hard to obtain or have a reputation for durability and reliability.

SERVICING

A car that is easy to maintain runs up only small servicing bills at your local garage and some jobs can be done at home; more complicated cars take up more time, so bills are steeper.

INSURANCE

Ordinary, simple cars are cheaper to insure than more exotic models with expensive spare parts.

DEPRECIATION

This is one of the biggest 'invisible' costs of running a car, and the more expensive the car the greater depreciation will be. A car depreciates more in its first year than at any other time – usually about one-fifth of its showroom cost. After two years it depreciates by about one-third of its original cost, and after three years by half. Unless mileages are huge, depreciation is not greatly influenced by the odometer reading (mileage): age of the car is the main criterion.

To average depreciation over the useful life of a car (about eight years, according to the AA) allow an annual figure of about $12\frac{1}{2}$ per cent loss – £200 a year on a car that is £1600 when new.

OTHER COSTS

To cut motoring costs noticeably it is important to consider all costs, not just those of running the car. Using an automatic car wash once a week, for example, greatly adds to your yearly costs; spending 10p a work-day on parking is worth as much in a year as the £25 road fund licence; and if you pay 25p a day at a station carpark that's worth as much petrol, over a working year, as you need to cover a third of the year's total mileage.

Use the table below* (which includes a hypothetical example) to calculate your own motoring costs for the year. Then you can see where possible savings can be made.

* Adapted from annual *AA Schedule of Running Costs*.

ANNUAL STANDING CHARGES	Example for typical 1600cc 2-year-old car	Your car
Road fund licence	£25	£25
Depreciation (allow approx. one-eighth of original value per year)	200	£
Insurance	70	£
Driving licence	0.33	£0.33
Motoring club membership	5.50	£
Garage rates or rent	10	£
Interest lost on capital invested in car (allow about 5 per cent of the car's current value)	70	£
	£380.83 per year	£ per year
For average per week divide by 52	£7.32	£
For average per mile divide by number of miles (e.g. 10 000) 380.83÷10 000	3.8p per mile	p per mile

RUNNING COSTS	Example based on 10 000 miles per year	
340 gallons petrol at 75p a gallon	£255	£
Oil	10	£
Tyres	25	£
Servicing	20	£
Repairs	50	£
Parking costs, fines	25	£
Polish	1	£
Weekly car wash	5	£
	£391 per year	£ per year
For cost per week divide by 52	£7.52	£
Cost per mile (over 10 000 miles)	3.9	p
TOTAL COST PER YEAR	£771.83	£
TOTAL COST PER WEEK	£14.84	£
TOTAL COST PER MILE	7.7p	p

There's no mystery about the sort of petrol consumption figures achieved in economy trials — Mini Clubman: 51 mpg; Escort 1300: 41 mpg; BLMC 1300: 44 mpg; Granada automatic: 25 mpg. It's delicate, tip-toe driving that does it and there is a lesson in it for everyone, even if it's only a question of how to get home on your last gallon of petrol.

MORE MILES FOR THE MONEY

Economy driving is concerned with all parts of the car, not only with how much petrol is sucked into the cylinders from the carburettor. For the ordinary motorist the art of saving money in motoring starts in his garage — with regular servicing and routine checks that ensure the car is running sweetly and efficiently.

TYRES

If tyre pressures are insufficient the car will have to strain more and will handle badly, so more petrol will be used and the tyres will wear out more quickly. A set of tyres should last about 20 000 miles.

WHEELS

If the wheels are out of alignment wear on the tyres is increased and engine power is wasted.

BRAKES

Check that the handbrake does not cause the back wheels to drag. All brakes should operate smoothly and firmly so that driving can be efficient.

BATTERY

A fading battery wastes petrol. The battery should always be in tip-top order and charged or replaced when it begins to deteriorate. A sensible plan is to change batteries every three years.

PETROL

Use the correct petrol for your car. A lower octane than that recommended by your handbook might be cheaper but can prove to be a false economy because in some circumstances it damages the engine. A higher octane is no advantage and is therefore a waste of money.

CHOKE

Use the choke as little as possible. After starting the engine move away immediately — do not race it to warm it up — and push the choke home as soon as you can.

LUGGAGE

Keep luggage inside the car — a roofrack loaded with suitcases imposes so much drag on a car that fuel consumption goes up by more than 5 per cent.

TEMPERATURE

Make sure the engine is running at its optimum temperature: sometimes a radiator blind is required to block off some of the cold air streaming through the radiator.

POLISH

Depreciation is lessened if the car is kept in good condition. Wash regularly with plain water (don't waste money on car shampoos) and polish sparingly.

SERVICING

Months can sometimes elapse before a car is given a routine inspection which will show up potential problems such as leaking oil seals. It is important to have the car serviced every three months at least, whatever its mileage.

SHORT JOURNEYS

The car must be used intelligently. Nothing contributes more to engine wear than short trips during which the engine has no time to get warm and circulate the oil fully through it. A succession of short trips can mean that the cylinders are never fully lubricated. If you want to move the car out of the garage to wash it, then push it out — don't start up if you can avoid it.

DRIVING

Economical driving is smooth and quiet. The pedals should be treated as if they were made of wood, and liable to snap off; pretend that the accelerator is a match-stick.

This means you have to look a long way ahead and anticipate what traffic will do. Avoid sudden stops — slow down gradually and smoothly. Hang well back from other traffic so sudden stops can be avoided. Harsh braking uses as much petrol as hard acceleration.

Don't pull away from a standing start as if it were the starting grid at Le Mans. Drive the car as if you were creeping away from a funeral before the end of a service. Be positive, don't annoy other traffic, but take it quietly and avoid revving the engine unnecessarily.

Stay in top gear as much as possible without straining the engine, avoid dabbing the accelerator between gears when changing up or down and, if you do have to change down on a hill, keep revs as low as is consistent with the need for speed.

Gunning the engine while stationary at traffic lights is a complete waste of petrol, you may as well pour it out of the window. Switch off if delays are going to be prolonged; however, a lot of stopping and starting imposes different kinds of expensive wear on the engine.

If the car is serviced regularly, spark plugs, points and carburettor should always be in good condition and properly adjusted. If they are not adjusted correctly the car can use 20 per cent more fuel without the driver's noticing any deterioration in performance.

When switching off the engine do not increase revs. This is an old-fashioned practice which has no use whatever in modern cars and serves only to waste petrol and wash oil off the sides of the cylinders, so increasing engine wear.

ECONOMY CHECK

△ Is the car running sweetly and smoothly?
△ Don't skimp on servicing, it's a false economy.
△ Use the correct star-rating of petrol for the car.
△ Use the choke sparingly.
△ Drive delicately: avoid speedy starts, hard stops.

ECONOMY DRIVING

These were the consumption figures achieved in the 1974 Mobil Economy Run:

Mini Clubman	51 mpg
Fiat 127	47 mpg
Imp Sport	47 mpg
Datsun Cherry 100A	46 mpg
Mini 850	46 mpg
Renault 5TL	46 mpg
Austin 1300	45 mpg
Simca 1100GLS	42 mpg
Austin 1100	42 mpg
Toledo	41 mpg
Escort 1300	41 mpg
Renault 12TL	40 mpg
Marina 1.3	37 mpg
Viva	37 mpg
Toyota Celica	41 mpg
Avenger	40 mpg
Opel Ascona 1.6S	39 mpg
Capri 1600	38 mpg
Maxi 1750	38 mpg
Hunter GL	37 mpg
Cortina 1600	36 mpg
VW K70	36 mpg
Marina 1.8	40 mpg
Triumph Dolomite	39 mpg
Audi 100LS	34 mpg
Cortina 2000GT	32 mpg
Consul	29 mpg
Mazda RX3	24 mpg
Marina 1.8 automatic	34 mpg
Scimitar GTE automatic	27 mpg
Granada automatic	25 mpg
Capri 3000GXL automatic	28 mpg
Cortina 1600 automatic	32 mpg
Ventora automatic	23 mpg
Jaguar XJ12 automatic	14 mpg
Daf 66 automatic	37 mpg

PART II
HOW YOUR CAR
WORKS

The motorist who knows a little of what goes on under the bonnet of his car is not only better informed, he is a better driver. Abuse of the car stems mainly from ignorance. No driver who understands how his clutch works, for example, will burn it out by holding the car on a hill because he is too lazy to use the handbrake! This section is a simple guide to how a car works. The illustrations on these two pages are keyed to the explanations on the following pages.

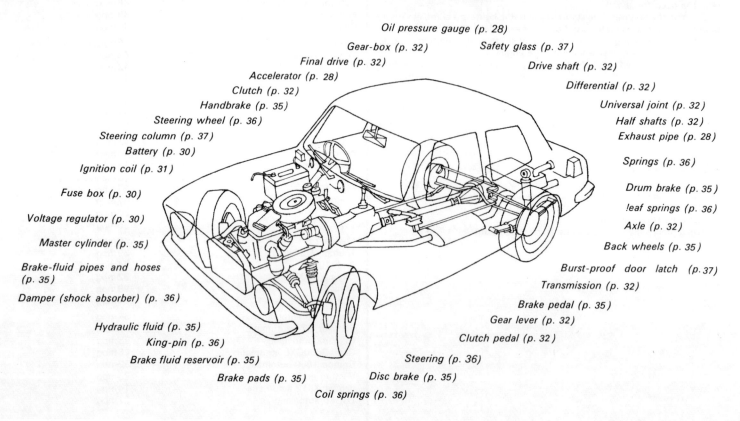

Oil pressure gauge (p. 28)

Gear-box (p. 32)

Safety glass (p. 37)

Final drive (p. 32)

Drive shaft (p. 32)

Accelerator (p. 28)

Differential (p. 32)

Clutch (p. 32)

Universal joint (p. 32)

Handbrake (p. 35)

Half shafts (p. 32)

Steering wheel (p. 36)

Exhaust pipe (p. 28)

Steering column (p. 37)

Battery (p. 30)

Springs (p. 36)

Ignition coil (p. 31)

Drum brake (p. 35)

Fuse box (p. 30)

!eaf springs (p. 36)

Voltage regulator (p. 30)

Axle (p. 32)

Master cylinder (p. 35)

Back wheels (p. 35)

Brake-fluid pipes and hoses (p. 35)

Burst-proof door latch (p. 37)

Damper (shock absorber) (p. 36)

Transmission (p. 32)

Brake pedal (p. 35)

Gear lever (p. 32)

Hydraulic fluid (p. 35)

Clutch pedal (p. 32)

King-pin (p. 36)

Steering (p. 36)

Brake fluid reservoir (p. 35)

Brake pads (p. 35)

Disc brake (p. 35)

Coil springs (p. 36)

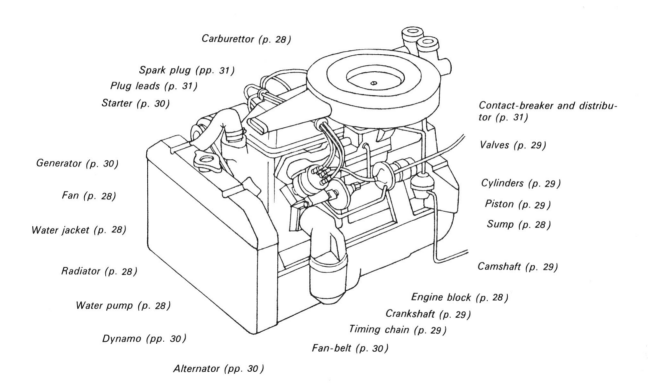

Carburettor (p. 28)

Spark plug (pp. 31)

Plug leads (p. 31)

Starter (p. 30)

Contact-breaker and distributor (p. 31)

Valves (p. 29)

Generator (p. 30)

Cylinders (p. 29)

Fan (p. 28)

Piston (p. 29)

Water jacket (p. 28)

Sump (p. 28)

Radiator (p. 28)

Camshaft (p. 29)

Water pump (p. 28)

Engine block (p. 28)

Crankshaft (p. 29)

Timing chain (p. 29)

Dynamo (pp. 30)

Fan-belt (p. 30)

Alternator (pp. 30)

WHAT MAKES IT TICK?

If you put a drop of petrol in a saucer and light it stand well back – it goes off with a huge flame. You can imagine the effect in a small space. The combustion of the petrol creates enormous energy, which is what drives the engine.

In a car engine this happens in the cylinder, which is a smooth hole bored in the engine block, usually made of cast iron, that forms the bulk of the engine. Moving up and down inside the cylinder is a piston.

A mixture of petrol vapour and air is sucked into the top of the cylinder from the carburettor and ignited by the spark plug. The combustion forces the piston sharply downward and this causes the crankshaft to turn and brings another piston up for its power stroke. Successive explosions in the cylinders cause the crankshaft to continue turning evenly, and this movement is transmitted through the clutch and gear-box to the wheels of the car.

Most family saloon cars have four, six or eight cylinders. Each piston has a cycle of four strokes. As the piston moves up following the first downward power stroke it pushes gases from the explosion out of the cylinder into the exhaust pipe. As it moves down again it sucks in a mixture of petrol and air from the carburettor. And as it comes up again this mixture is compressed ready for another spark to ignite it. When the car is idling the cycle is repeated about twelve times a second, at full power about 100 times a second.

When the crankshaft turns it also drives the timing chain, which turns a camshaft on top of the engine, or on one side of it. This allows the inlet and outlet valves in the top of each cylinder to open and shut in strict order, allowing petrol to be sucked in, the cylinder to be closed and exhaust gases pushed out in rotation.

When the accelerator is depressed half an inch the movement is fed through levers to the carburettor, which opens a little to allow more petrol vapour to be sucked into each cylinder, causing bigger explosions and giving more power.

This 'internal combustion' causes enormous heat – about 700°F – so the engine is surrounded by a jacket filled with water which is circulated by a water pump and cooled by a fan and by air rushing through the radiator.

To prevent friction between the 150 fast-moving metal parts in the engine they are lubricated by oil which is pumped under pressure throughout the engine and allowed to drain down into the sump, from where it is recirculated.

The last link in the chain is the electrical system. When the engine turns it also drives the dynamo or alternator, which recharges the battery for the next time you start the engine, and provides electricity to the rest of the car. High-voltage power produced by the ignition coil is led to the distributor, which sends a spark to each cylinder at just the right instant.

EFFICIENCY CHECKS

An engine is a highly complicated apparatus which is at its best only when fed the right diet of petrol, oil, water and air designed for it. This is why it is important to read your car handbook to ensure the car is using:

△ The right petrol – use only the octanes recommended.

△ The right mixture – the carburettor mixes petrol with air. This mixture is critical, so the carburettor must always be in good working order.

△ The right oil – the film of lubricant sandwiched between rapidly moving metal parts is all important, so good oil is one luxury an engine really deserves.

△ The right oil pressure – if your car has an oil pressure gauge you can check that the oil is being distributed properly to all the moving parts of the engine. If oil pressure drops, switch off and check oil level (see p. 42).

△ The right temperature – very cold air can make an engine run inefficiently, but if the engine gets too hot, because of lack of water, big trouble results.

Spark explodes the petrol mixture, forcing the piston down so the crankshaft turns, bringing the next piston up into position.

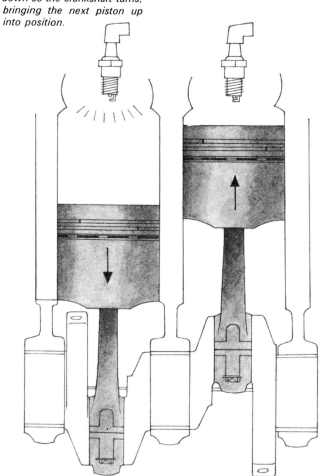

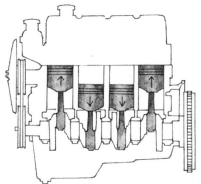

As the crankshaft turns it drives the wheels and allows other pistons to blow out exhaust gases and suck in petrol.

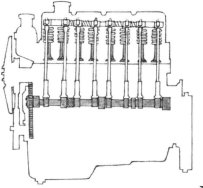

The front end of the crankshaft drives a timing chain which turns a camshaft that lets the valves in the top of each cylinder open and shut in order.

WHAT MAKES IT START?

Electrics are the nerves of the car, in the sense that they trigger off the chain of events that culminates in the wheels being driven round. And the core of the electrical system, every bit as important to the car as the spinal cord is to the body, is the ignition.

The car's power station is the battery and generator, which take over from each other depending on whether the car is idling or running fast. The ignition system continuously feeds the electricity from the battery or generator to each of the cylinders, boosting it on the way to more than a thousand times its voltage so that a spark will cause the petrol in each cylinder to ignite at just the right fraction of a second.

Ignition problems cause more breakdowns than anything else, but the ignition system itself is perfectly reliable if properly maintained. In nearly every case ignition trouble can be traced to damp, dirt or lack of servicing. A car's electrical system can be impaired by bad connections which prevent the full amount of current from surging through.

Electric power is measured in two ways: as *current*, which is the amount of energy available (the amount of water in the pipe), and as *voltage*, which is the pressure (like the pressure which makes water squirt out of taps).

When a fuse blows it is like a pipe bursting, except that it is designed to happen in a certain place before damage is done elsewhere. If a fuse is not fitted the wires could become so hot that they catch fire.

Other electrical circuits in the car operate headlights, brake lights, warning lights, wipers, horn, indicators, heater and other components. Some parts are connected on the same circuit, like the ring main of a house, and are protected by the same fuse.

Sometimes bulbs or working parts fail, or bad connections cause the circuit to fail, but in general these electrical circuits are simple to understand and to check, and are reliable if kept in good condition.

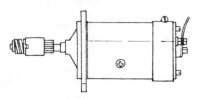

1 STARTER MOTOR

A powerful electric motor fixed to the side of the engine, it drains as much power out of the battery when turning the engine as seventy headlamps. Teeth on the end of the starter motor engage automatically with teeth on a large cogwheel attached to the crankshaft of the engine; as it turns, the entire mechanical system of the engine is set in motion so that the engine fires and begins to run of its own accord. The starter motor then automatically disengages.

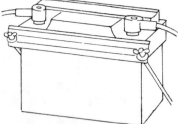

2 BATTERY

This stores the electricity required to turn the starter motor and to supply the ignition system when the engine is idling. It acts like a water cistern: power is drained when it is required to start the engine, then it is topped up by the generator ready for the next time. It gives no trouble if kept in good condition with the terminal connections firm and clean.

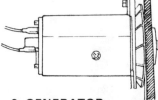

3 GENERATOR

There are two types: the dynamo, which recharges the battery only when the engine is running fast so the battery has to supply all the needs of the car – ignition, headlights, radio, wipers; the alternator, which is more expensive but increasingly popular because it supplies current even at slow speeds. The purpose of these is to generate electricity to be stored in the battery. They are turned by the fan-belt, which is driven by the engine.

4 VOLTAGE AND CURRENT REGULATOR

This is a small sealed unit, which generally lasts as long as the car, to ensure that the battery is not overcharged, that the generator is not damaged by high voltage and that the battery electricity does not leak away through the generator. It is often incorporated into an alternator casing, but is always separate when used with a dynamo.

THE IGNITION SYSTEM

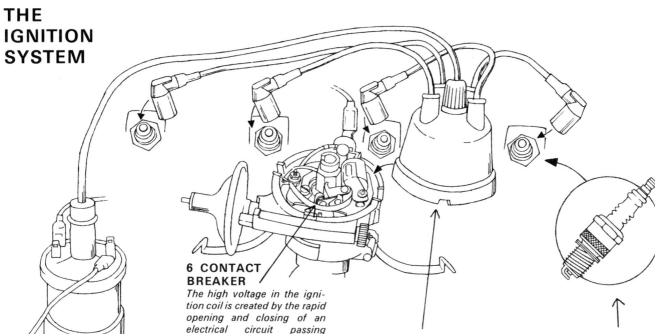

5 IGNITION COIL

When power is released by the battery it is only 12 volts. The ignition coil is a transformer which boosts it to the order of 15 000 volts so it has enough pressure to jump the gap at the end of a spark plug and create a spark. It is like putting your thumb over the end of a garden hose to achieve a stronger jet using the same amount of water.

6 CONTACT BREAKER

The high voltage in the ignition coil is created by the rapid opening and closing of an electrical circuit passing through it and affecting the magnetic field. To achieve this opening and closing, a shaft driven by the engine rotates between electrical points. Each time the circuit is broken – about 10 000 times a minute at 70 mph – a surge of high-voltage power is released by the ignition coil. The points wear out or become dirty easily and need regular attention (see p. 58), and are the biggest single cause of ignition trouble.

7 DISTRIBUTOR

The high-voltage current is fed along thickly insulated wire from the coil to the distributor, from which other wires lead to the spark plugs. Inside the distributor is a rotor which spins between the inside end of each lead so that pulses of power are distributed to each cylinder in turn. The distributor is particularly prone to dust contamination and dampness, as are the leads to the spark plugs.

8 SPARK PLUG

Probably the simplest part of the engine, it is screwed into the top of each cylinder and has an insulated ceramic top. The high-voltage current passes down the length of the plug and jumps across the gap at the end, causing the petrol mixture in the cylinder to ignite. The size of gap is critical for efficient running. Spark plugs should be kept clean and renewed every 10 000–12 000 miles.

WHAT MAKES IT GO?

The link between the engine and wheels is called the transmission. Its layout varies according to the type of car. A car can be driven by its front wheels, like a Mini, or in the conventional way by its back wheels, like any Ford car. It can also have its engine in the rear and be driven by its back wheels, like an NSU. Whatever the layout, the transmission has three main components.

CLUTCH

Operated by the foot on the clutch pedal, the clutch breaks the link between the engine and the gear-box, so the engine can turn freely without any strain on it. It works by friction, and comprises two plates which are pressed against each other by some kind of spring mechanism. When you depress the clutch the two plates are forced apart a fraction of an inch so they can spin independently. One plate is covered with a high-friction material like a brake lining, which wears out with use and has to be replaced. If you 'ride' the clutch by resting your foot on it when the car is moving the plates will slip and extra wear will result. If the car judders when the clutch is engaged it usually means the lining material has worn thin.

GEAR-BOX

When you change gear a metal arm inside the gear-box, operated by the gear lever, selects different sets of cogs. For first gear, when a lot of power is needed to get the car rolling, cogs are selected so the engine makes about fourteen revolutions for every single turn of the wheels. At top speed the momentum of the car means that not so much power is required, so the engine makes only four revolutions for every single turn of the wheels. The intermediate gears, second and third, have ratios of about eight to one and six to one.

FINAL DRIVE

In a conventional front-engine, rear-wheel-drive car the gear-box is linked to the wheels by a drive shaft, which is coupled by universal joints so it can tilt different ways as the car is affected by bumps and roll. The drive shaft leads to the differential, which is the large bulge on the axle between the rear wheels. This transmits driving power to the wheels, and also permits one rear wheel to travel faster than the other when the car goes round a bend. Like the gear-box it must be regularly topped up with oil, often of a special type (check handbook). In a front-wheel-drive car, or a rear-wheel-drive car with a rear-mounted engine, final drive and gear-box are part of the engine assembly and often lubricated by the same oil.

AUTOMATIC TRANSMISSION

Many cars have automatic clutches and gear-boxes. All you have to do is depress the accelerator to drive off, or the brake pedal to stop, and the engine automatically selects the correct gear. This is a simple and labour-saving way of driving. It tends to use more petrol but keeps the engine in better order because it is less prone to abuse. How it works is easily explained if you think of the way an egg-beater tends to make the mixing bowl spin round and round. An automatic clutch is filled with oil; the driving part of the engine is the egg-beater. When it runs slowly the bowl does not turn. As speed is increased the bowl turns faster and faster until ultimately it travels at the same speed as the egg-beater.

Three types of transmission:

1 Front-engine, rear-wheel-drive (Ford).

2 Front-engine, front-wheel-drive (Mini).

3 Rear-engine, rear-wheel-drive (Volkswagen).

CONVENTIONAL
TRANSMISSION
LAYOUT

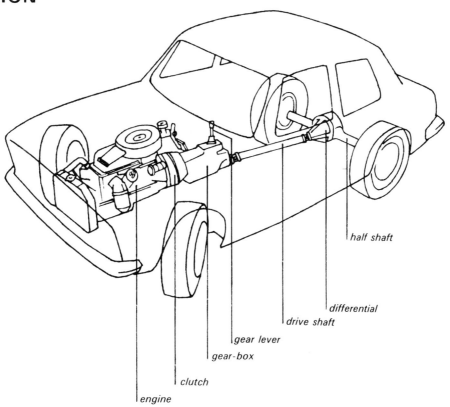

half shaft

differential

drive shaft

gear lever

gear-box

clutch

engine

WHAT MAKES IT STOP?

Many motorists boast of how fast their cars will go, but it's really much more impressive to talk about performance in terms of stopping power. The brakes do a much better job than the engine. A one-ton car can be stopped from 60 mph in under four seconds, and in that same length of time the brakes generate enough heat to boil three pints of water.

Brakes work by friction: when you push the brake pedal a pad of high-friction material containing asbestos is pressed with great force against a smooth metal plate attached to each wheel. There are two main types of brake: the drum brake, in which pressure is applied on the inside of what looks like a shallow casserole pan; the disc brake, in which friction pads pinch against a spinning metal disc.

Disc brakes are the more powerful because the disc is exposed to the slipstream of the car and does not get so hot. When a car brakes it tilts forward, throwing most of its weight on the front wheels. For this reason most modern cars have the more efficient disc brakes on the front wheels and drum brakes on the rear.

In the course of driving the friction material wears out. With careful motoring a set of brake pads for the front disc brakes lasts about 12 000 miles; the linings for drum brakes in the rear last a little longer. Some modern brakes are self-adjusting, so it is not necessary to make adjustments to them as pads or linings become thinner.

It is most important to keep a careful check on the condition of the brakes. If the friction material wears out the brakes become ineffective and metal rivets will score the drum or disc. The extra heat generated by thin friction pads can also cause brakes to fail.

Consistent braking – when you are going down a steep hill, for example – can cause brakes to 'fade', so they operate less and less efficiently. This is caused by heat in the friction material, and can be alleviated by applying the brakes on and off, or holding the car by changing to a lower gear so the brakes can rest and cool.

Wetness also affects brakes badly. After driving through a ford it is important to test the brakes hard; if they don't work drive a short distance with gentle pressure on the brake pedal so the friction material of the pads and linings is dried out by heat. Downpours of rain that make the roads run with water can also reduce the braking efficiency of some cars, particularly when motoring fast for long distances without using the brakes, as on motorways. In wet conditions it is important to test the brakes regularly and, if necessary, to slow down.

The handbrake works independently of the footbrake system and in most cars is linked only to the rear wheels. It may be used to stop the car in an emergency, applied cautiously because it is liable to lock the rear wheels and cause a skid. The quickest way to stop, using only the handbrake, is to jerk it firmly on and off.

Some cars have 'power assisted' brakes, in which a vacuum system applies extra force to the brakes when you use the brake pedal. This makes driving much lighter, and efficient braking does not rely so much on the driver's own muscle power.

CHECKING BRAKES FROM THE DRIVING SEAT

△ There should be little more than one inch of play in the pedal.

△ If brakes snatch, or pull to one side, they need urgent attention.

△ If the pedal feels 'spongy', and brake performance is improved when the pedal is pumped on and off, there is air or a leak in the hydraulic system.

IF YOUR BRAKES FAIL

△ Pump the brake pedal on and off, fast.

△ Change down through the gears to slow the car.

△ Ease the handbrake on gently so the rear wheels do not lock, or snatch it on and off.

△ Do your best to steer out of trouble.

△ If there is time, put on hazard lights, headlights, and sound the horn.

HANDBRAKE

The handbrake is linked to the rear brake drums or discs by a mechanical linkage and is designed to be used mainly when the car is stationary.

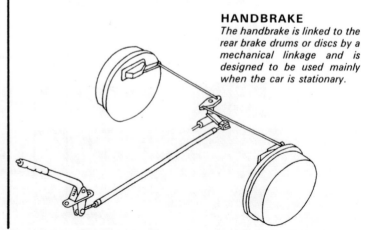

BRAKE-FLUID RESERVOIR

The all-important fluid in the brake system is automatically topped up from this small container, which in many modern cars is transparent so its level can be checked at a glance. Checks should be made once a week.

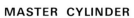

MASTER CYLINDER

When the brake pedal is depressed it pushes a piston inside this cylinder which exerts pressure on the hydraulic fluid in the tubes leading to the brake on each wheel.

BRAKE PEDAL

There should be little more than one inch of play in the brake pedal: if there is any more the brakes may need adjusting.

BRAKE FLUID

A synthetic fluid designed not to corrode rubber (as oil products do), this is the vital component of the whole system. It has a high boiling point so the heat of the brakes does not cause it to boil. If it does boil it changes into vapour which compresses under pressure and the brakes fail. It is important to use only the brake fluid specified in the car's handbook. The hydraulic system should be flushed through with fresh brake fluid every eighteen months or 18 000 miles. This is because over a period of time it absorbs water, which drastically reduces the boiling point. Use brake fluid only from a newly opened container, and take care not to shake it up thereby introducing air bubbles.

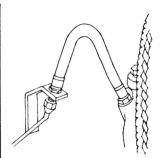

BRAKE-FLUID TUBES AND HOSES

The pressure applied to the hydraulic fluid by the master cylinder is carried to the brakes by these tubes, some of which must be flexible to allow for steering movements and wheel-travel over bumps. They take a considerable pounding from stones, and because they are beneath the car the steel tubes are susceptible to corrosion from salt. They must not only prevent leaks against considerable pressure, but must also prevent air from entering the system, for this can cause complete brake failure. The system must be regularly inspected and all rubber seals and hoses replaced every three years or 40 000 miles.

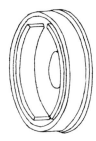

DRUM BRAKE

The friction material, or 'lining', is riveted to semi-circular shoes inside the spinning metal drum. Pressure on the hydraulic fluid causes the shoes to move outwards and rub against the inside of the drum.

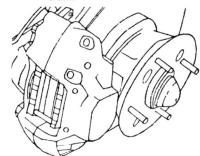

DISC BRAKE

Pressure on the hydraulic fluid causes piston-operated calipers to squeeze the brake pads against the smooth metal disc which spins with the wheel. The pads should be replaced when two-thirds worn down (see p. 34).

WHAT KEEPS IT ON THE ROAD?

Suspension is the system of springs that absorbs the bumps in the road. Steering is the means of directing the car in a required direction. Suspension and steering interrelate because they both affect the front wheels simultaneously. When a car takes a bend at speed enormous centrifugal forces are created. Suspension and steering must overcome these forces, not only keeping the car on the road and making it comfortable for people to ride in, but keeping the car at the right point of balance so it does not roll over.

STEERING

Most popular cars have rack and pinion steering, which is precise and easy to handle. It comprises a toothed bar, or rack, which is moved one way or the other by a cog that is revolved by means of the steering column. The sideways movement of the rack turns the wheels, which are kept nearly parallel.

The front wheels of rear-wheel-drive cars point very slightly inwards (toe-in); on front-wheel-drive cars they usually point slightly outwards (toe-out). If toe-in or toe-out becomes excessive it causes the tyres to scuff, leaving tell-tale marks on the tread. The alignment of the wheels should then be checked with special equipment available in most big garages. The swivels, or king-pins, on which the front wheels turn are angled so that when the steering wheel is released while the car is moving it will automatically straighten up.

Some big cars are fitted with power-assisted steering to make steering lighter, particularly at slow speeds when parking. If the system fails the car can still be steered in the normal way, although more effort is needed. Complete power steering is avoided in cars because it does not allow the driver to 'feel' the road and sense the balance and adhesion of the car.

SUSPENSION

The suspension of a car works in the same way, in principle, as the springs inside a seat. The main difference is that the car also has dampers, often known as shock absorbers, which reduce the rebound effect of the springs.

Leaf springs, which tend to absorb bumps by deflection, are usually used on rear wheels. Coil springs, which compress, are usually used on the front wheels. Some have independent suspension, which means that any single wheel can move independently of the others. Some cars do not rely on springs at all, but on either oil, gas or water in sealed pipes which compresses to absorb the shock of a wheel rising over a bump and has the effect of raising the opposite end of the car so it is always level.

The effectiveness of any single suspension system varies considerably because a suspension that is ideal for the car carrying only the driver will be too soft for the same car loaded with passengers and luggage. Many estate cars have a much harder suspension, which gives passengers a rougher ride, and makes the car handle differently when there are only one or two people riding in it.

The suspension is designed to absorb not only bumps but also the higher frequencies of vibration caused by tyres running over such things as cobbles or grooved road surfaces. At the same time the suspension must be sturdy enough to withstand the stresses of hard braking and sharp cornering.

SAFETY CHECK

△ There should be less than $\frac{1}{2}$ in of free play in the steering wheel before the front wheels begin to move: more play indicates excessive wear.

△ To test the shock absorbers and springs, lean heavily on each corner of the car and release: the car should rise up, then bounce down and up once more only.

Rack and pinion steering is the simplest and most precise form of steering and is fitted to most popular cars.

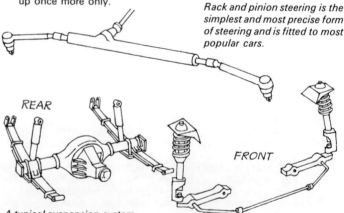

A typical suspension system — independent suspension on the front wheels with dampers (shock absorbers) and coil springs; leaf springs on the rear with telescopic dampers. The anti-roll bar lessens roll of the car's body when cornering.

WHAT MAKES IT SAFE?

Safety engineering is becoming more important in car design. In the past safety has traditionally taken a back seat to performance. Motor manufacturers believed that motorists would not pay money for safety. Now the car-buying public puts a greater emphasis on the safety qualities of cars, and this attitude is encouraged and reinforced by government legislation. The motoring organisations, particularly the AA, take a strong interest in safety and members have access to its reports on the safety features of particular models.

Safety is tackled on two main fronts:

PRIMARY SAFETY

Primary safety is the ability of a car to avoid an accident in the first place. It is the total of its good qualities and its ability to forgive the driver's mistakes. In other words, if the driver takes a bend too fast and loses his nerve, standing hard on the brakes, will the car slow down and stay on course or will it spin off the road or overturn? If the driver has to take swift avoiding action, will the car be light and precise to control and go where the driver directs it?

Primary safety must be designed into the car at the drawing-board stage, it can't be added on later. It includes all aspects of car handling: strong reliable brakes; precise and light steering; good suspension; good visibility with no blind spots; good stability resistant to cross-winds, etc. Because they are more manoeuvrable, nippier, and lighter to handle, European cars in general are very much safer in these respects than American cars, which are designed mainly for long fast journeys on straight flat roads.

SECONDARY SAFETY

If a car does have an accident, how can the occupants be protected from injury? – this is secondary safety. It includes such things as seatbelts, dashboard padding, and door latches which will not burst open and allow the car's inhabitants to fly out on to the road.

In an accident such as a head-on collision the car stops dead while its occupants carry on travelling at the same speed as before until they hit something. The aim of the engineer is to build into the car a system of progressive collapse of different parts so the occupants are slowed down with as little injury as possible before they hit something immovable.

The first stage in the chain of events is the stretch, or 'ride down', built into the seatbelt. In a 30 mph accident all seatbelts stretch by about 15 per cent so the wearer's body is slowed down progressively. Even if the seatbelt then breaks it doesn't matter because it has done its job.

By law, all new steering columns are designed to collapse, or be deflected, so they do little harm if a driver hits one with his chest. The rim of the steering wheel should not be so strong that if a driver hits it with his head he is seriously hurt. Engineers also give consideration to the area under the dashboard which occupants will hit with their knees. The fascia area is padded with thick foam to prevent serious injury. Switches should not stick out of the dashboard like a bed of nails but be recessed or flat in shape. There should be no jagged edges which could cause injury in an accident, e.g. sharp-edged rear-vision mirrors or window-winders.

Many windscreens are of toughened glass which shatters on impact forming smooth-edged granules that may cut the face in an accident but will not cause serious injury. Also the windscreen becomes opaque, seriously limiting visibility. It can happen in a split second and be very startling, particularly when taking a bend at speed. Laminated glass is much better but more expensive: it cracks when struck by a stone but does not shiver into a thousand fragments and you can usually carry on driving for some time without getting a new windscreen fitted.

Some cars are designed so the occupants are protected by a steel cage which does not collapse, and which prevents the engine and other parts of the car from intruding.

These aspects of car design are comparatively in their infancy, and safety education of motorists together with pressure from consumer organisations such as the AA will compel a much more sophisticated approach to car-occupant safety in the cars of tomorrow.

HOW SECONDARY SAFETY PROTECTS CAR OCCUPANTS

PART III
LOOKING AFTER
YOUR CAR

Regular servicing of the car is essential. If not serviced a car may use more than 20 per cent more petrol with no marked deterioration in performance. Moving parts will wear out more quickly. Most importantly, it will become a safety hazard.

The need to spend a few pounds every few weeks is irksome, but it saves hundreds of pounds in the long run.

Much of the servicing routine is simple and owners can save garage labour charges by doing it themselves. But don't hesitate to get the job done professionally if safety is at stake. If doubtful about the brakes or steering, have them checked by a garage.

In any case, it is a useful check to have the car fully serviced by a garage at least once a year. Ask for a full safety check of steering (wear, wheel alignment), brakes, suspension and body corrosion. Additional servicing is required for automatic transmission, power steering, servo-assisted brakes and high-performance engines.

This section covers most servicing jobs that can be carried out at home on simple cars. However, it is not possible to include the many variations for different cars.

USE THIS BOOK AND ITS CHECKLISTS IN CONJUNCTION WITH YOUR CAR HANDBOOK.

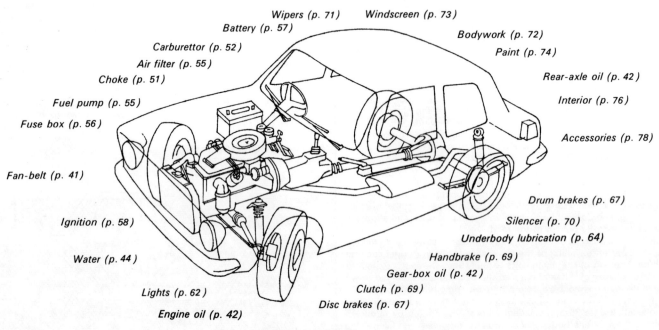

Wipers (p. 71)
Windscreen (p. 73)
Battery (p. 57)
Bodywork (p. 72)
Carburettor (p. 52)
Paint (p. 74)
Air filter (p. 55)
Choke (p. 51)
Rear-axle oil (p. 42)
Fuel pump (p. 55)
Interior (p. 76)
Fuse box (p. 56)
Accessories (p. 78)
Fan-belt (p. 41)
Drum brakes (p. 67)
Ignition (p. 58)
Silencer (p. 70)
Underbody lubrication (p. 64)
Water (p. 44)
Handbrake (p. 69)
Gear-box oil (p. 42)
Lights (p. 62)
Clutch (p. 69)
Disc brakes (p. 67)
Engine oil (p. 42)
Tyres (pp. 46—49)

DO-IT-YOURSELF SERVICING

DAILY

△ Check radiator water (p. 44).
△ Check tyre pressures, inspect for tyre damage (p. 46).
△ Check engine oil (p. 42).
△ Check hydraulic-fluid reservoirs (p. 66).
△ Clean windscreen (p. 73).

WEEKLY

Carry out all daily checks plus:

△ Check battery water level and connections (p. 57).
△ Fill windscreen washer (p. 45).
△ Check tyre treads for wear (p 46).
△ Check for leaks of oil, water, hydraulic fluid (p.44 45 68).
△ Check brake efficiency, adjust if necessary (p. 66).
△ Check all electric bulbs and controls working (p. 62).
△ Wash car (p. 72).

THREE-MONTHLY (OR EVERY 3000 MILES)

Carry out all daily and weekly checks plus:

△ Change engine oil (p. 43).
△ Check contact-breaker points (p. 58).
△ Check and clean distributor, cap, leads, coil (p. 58).
△ Check fan-belt tension (p. 41).
△ Check gear-box oil (p. 42).
△ Check rear-axle oil (p. 42).
△ Check and adjust clutch travel (p. 69).
△ Top up carburettor piston damper (if fitted) (p. 52).
△ Check brake hoses for wear or corrosion (p. 66).
△ Adjust handbrake (p. 69).
△ Grease lubrication nipples (p. 65).
△ Check headlamp alignment (p. 63).
△ Oil pedal linkages, door and boot hinges, etc (p. 77).

SIX-MONTHLY (OR EVERY 6000 MILES)

Carry out all checks listed above plus:

△ Renew engine-oil filter (p. 43).
△ Renew contact-breaker points (p. 58).
△ Check carburettor setting (p. 52).
△ Inspect and dust brake linings (p. 67).
△ Check exhaust pipe and mountings (p. 70).
△ Check anti-freeze mixture (p. 44).

ANNUAL (OR EVERY 12000 MILES)

Carry out all checks listed above plus:

△ Renew or clean air filter (p. 55).
△ Check seatbelts for wear (p. 77).
△ Replace windscreen-wiper blades (p. 71).
△ Replace spark plugs (p. 60).

COMPARE THIS LIST WITH SERVICING CHART IN YOUR CAR HANDBOOK

TOOLKIT

A set of tools sufficient to do most of the jobs mentioned in this book is not expensive, but it is worth buying good-quality tools because they will last a lifetime and are less likely to cause damage. This set can be carried easily in a small box or wrapped in canvas in the boot of the car.

Tyre-pressure gauge
Tyre-tread depth gauge
Jack
Wheelbrace
Torch and/or engine light
Oil-can
High-pressure grease-gun
Small ball hammer (about $\frac{3}{4}$ lb)
Small file
Set of feeler gauges
Wire brush
Insulated general-purpose pliers with cutters
Spark-plug spanner
Electrical-circuit tester
2 jump leads
Spanners: Set of combination and ring spanners to match the type of nuts
and bolts of your car (refer to handbook)
Screwdrivers: Large engineering screwdriver
Small electrics screwdriver
Medium general-purpose screwdriver
Medium cross-head screwdriver
Small cross-head screwdriver
Small tin of touch-up paint
Small paintbrush
Hydrometer
Insulating tape
Wet-and-dry emery paper

NEED AT HOME
Plastic bottle or syringe
Drip bowl or tray to catch oil
Soft chamois leather

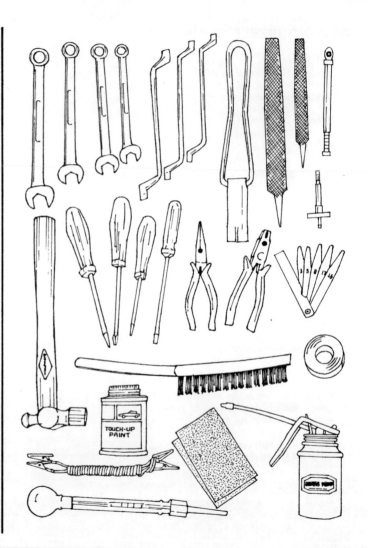

SPARE PARTS

If a car is serviced regularly it should not break down, and if it does break down most spare parts are readily obtainable from motoring club patrols or garages. When you go abroad kits of spare parts can be hired at modest cost and any parts used are charged on return.

ALWAYS CARRY IN THE CAR

△ Tow rope
△ Fan-belt
△ Fuses
△ Spare petrol in leak-proof can
△ Spare ignition/door key wired to a concealed place under the wing or engine of the car
△ Chains (if snowy conditions)

△ Red warning triangle
△ Large dry rag
△ Water-repellent spray
△ De-icing spray

WHEN GOING ABROAD ALSO CARRY

Sealed-beam headlight unit or bulbs
Bulbs for side, tail, brake and indicator lights
Tyre valve cores
Set of points
Set of spark plugs
Condenser for distributor
Rotor arm
Ignition coil

Fuel pump
Top and bottom radiator hoses
Length of high-tension lead
Small coil of insulated wire
Plastic emergency windscreen

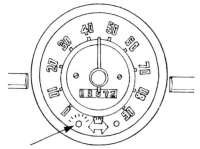

The first warning that the fan-belt is broken is the red ignition light coming on, indicating that the generator is no longer charging the battery. Stop and check the fan-belt immediately.

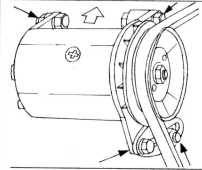

Slacken the generator positioning bolts and slide the generator towards the engine. Fit the belt over the fan and position it on the pulleys.

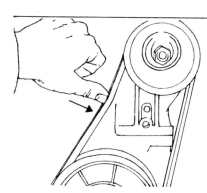

CHANGING THE FAN-BELT

The fan-belt is important because it often drives the generator and the water pump as well as the fan. There should be about $\frac{3}{4}$ in of play in the belt's longest side when it is pressed.

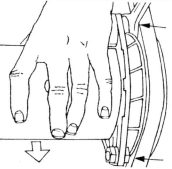

Swing the generator outwards until there is $\frac{3}{4}$ in play in the longest side of the fan-belt, then tighten the nuts to hold the generator in position.

OIL

The lower part of the engine is filled with oil which, as soon as the engine starts, is circulated under pressure to all moving parts and up to the top of the engine, from where it trickles down again to the sump.

The oil serves two vital functions. It forms a film between moving metal parts to stop their rubbing against each other, and it absorbs the heat generated by fast-moving components. Without oil the moving parts become white hot and fuse together.

A pint of oil lasts between 600 and 2000 miles. At three-monthly intervals or 3000 miles, all the engine oil must be changed. Oil is available in different grades to suit hot or cold climates, but most cars use 'multi-grade'. It is important to use only the type of oil specified in your car handbook.

Dispose of oil only at a garage or at a special local authority disposal facility. Tipping it down the drain is illegal; burying it is an ecological disaster.

Keep a constant watch for oil leaks around the engine, transmission and wheel hubs. After changing oil run the engine for a short time, then check for leaks. Look for oil stains on the road where the car has been parked.

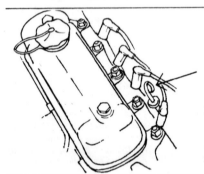

CHECKING THE ENGINE OIL

Engine oil should be checked daily. The engine must be cold and the car level. Remove the dipstick, wipe it with a cloth, make sure it is fully seated, then withdraw it.

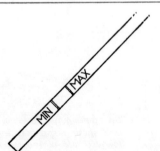

If the oil is below the lower mark on the dipstick top it up a little at a time, allowing time for the oil to drain down. Do not over-fill.

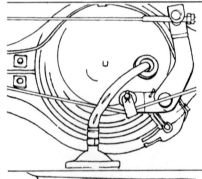

CHECKING REAR-AXLE OIL

Remove the plug halfway up the differential housing. Top up with correct oil, using plastic bottle or oil syringe, until oil reaches level of hole. Allow excess to drain, then replace plug.

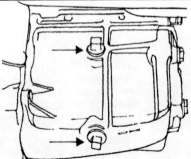

CHECKING THE GEAR-BOX OIL

Oil level should be up to level of the upper plug on the side of the gear-box. When changing oil use lower plug to drain gear-box, first slackening upper nut so air can enter. Use only the correct oil.

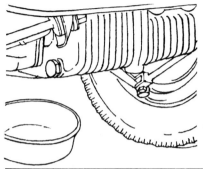

CHANGING THE ENGINE OIL

Run the engine to normal temperature, park on level ground, switch off. Slide bowl or tray underneath to catch waste oil. Remove oil-filler cap.

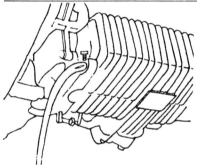

Taking care not to damage the nut, undo the sump drain plug so engine oil drains out into container. Some plugs are magnetic to catch metal fragments and require wiping clean.

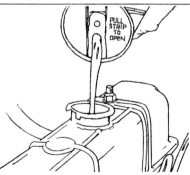

Replace nut and fill with correct amount of the right type of oil (see car handbook). Check dipstick. After running the engine check that the sump plug is not leaking. Dispose of oil in a garage or special local authority disposal facility.

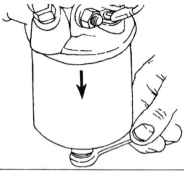

RENEWING THE OIL FILTER

Unscrew the retaining bolt a few turns and pull the casing down to break the seal. Hold a drip tray underneath as some oil will spill. Remove the unit fully and pull filter out of the casing.

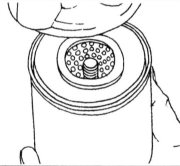

Wipe old oil out of the casing with a clean cloth and insert new filter. Use small screwdriver to remove sealing ring from the filter connection mounted on the engine. Insert new seal, replace unit, check dipstick.

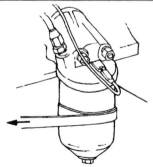

Some oil filters are of the canister type of which the whole unit is disposable. If you have trouble unscrewing it loop a strap around the body. When the job is complete: top up, run the engine, check for leaks.

WATER

The engine is kept at proper working temperature by water which is pumped around it, and the water in turn is cooled by air flowing through the radiator. The water pump of a middle-sized car pushes 18 gallons of water through the cooling system every minute; it is driven by the fan-belt, which must be properly adjusted and not worn. An over-heating engine could be due to:

△ Broken fan belt.
△ Low water level due to leaking radiator cap, radiator or radiator hoses.
△ Broken water pump.
△ Thermostat out of order.

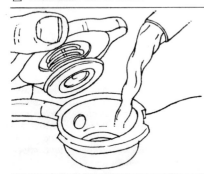

TOPPING UP
Regular checks of the water level are essential. If the engine is hot, use a cloth to cover the radiator cap and remove slowly at arm's length; wait until the engine cools before topping up.

TESTING ANTI-FREEZE
Test the anti-freeze by draining a little into a cup and storing it overnight in the freezer compartment of a fridge: if it remains liquid and does not freeze it does not need replacing.

ANTI-FREEZE

Anti-freeze is a chemical compound which is mixed with the radiator water to prevent it freezing in cold weather; it also contains anti-corrosion compounds to protect the inside of the radiator and the cooling jacket.

The correct proportion of anti-freeze to water is listed in your handbook; greater concentrations may be required in very cold regions. The anti-freeze can remain in the system all year round but should be replaced every two years.

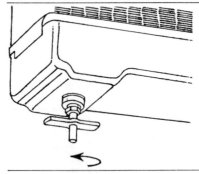

DRAINING AND CLEANING
For draining the cooling system there is usually a tap or plug at the bottom of the radiator. If the radiator contains anti-freeze less than one year old it can be collected in a can and used again.

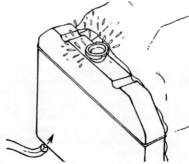

As dirt tends to collect in radiators from the top they can be flushed out by squirting a garden water hose upwards through the tap or bottom-hose connection; cover the engine to keep it dry.

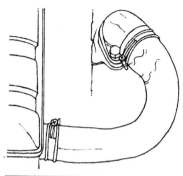

REPLACING A RADIATOR HOSE

Radiator hoses, subject to pressure, vibration and heat, deteriorate with age. Keep a regular watch for the tell-tale, pale-coloured stains that denote a leaking hose.

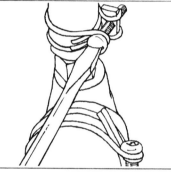

To replace a hose first drain the water until the level is below that of the hose. Unscrew the clips at either end, then work the hose free.

The ends of the new hose should overlap the connecting pipes by at least 1 in. After tightening the clips fill the radiator and run the engine to test for leaks.

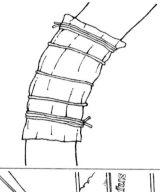

EMERGENCY REPAIRS

A leaking radiator hose can be repaired temporarily by binding it with a plastic bag which in turn is bound with wire. Several layers of insulation tape will also get you to the next garage.

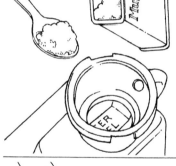

A leaking radiator can be temporarily plugged with a spoonful of dry mustard or oatmeal; at the first opportunity get a real radiator sealing compound at a garage or accessory shop.

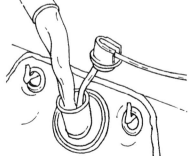

WINDSCREEN WASHER

Keep the windscreen washer fully topped up. Do not put in anti-freeze, which causes rubber seals and wiper blades to deteriorate. A spoonful of ammonia in the water will reduce windscreen smear.

AIR

The amount of air inside the tyres of a medium-sized family saloon car weighs only about two and a half ounces, but as far as safety and performance are concerned it is one of the most critical of all the car's components. The pressure of the air inside the tyres must be exactly right (check manufacturer's specifications). If the pressure is not correct for the use to which the car is being put you are committing an offence — the police often do checks.

Insufficient tyre inflation causes the tyres to wear out quicker because they get hotter, increases fuel consumption because the wheels don't roll so easily, unbalances the car on corners and during braking, and in general is a serious hazard to other road-users.

Tyres must be inspected for damage and their pressures checked at frequent intervals. Pressures must be increased for fast motoring, towing or carrying heavy loads (check manufacturer's specifications). Do not rely on the air-pressure gauges fitted to garage air hoses but carry your own tyre pressure gauge. This can be tested for you by the Department of Trading Standards, which can be contacted through the local town hall.

Dust caps should always be placed on the valves to prevent grit from entering.

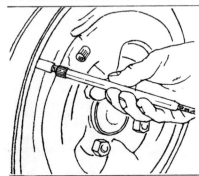

REGULAR TYRE-CARE CHECKS

Check air pressure daily, but only when the tyres are cold. Use your own pressure gauge and replace dust cap. Tyre pressure increases by about 4 lb per square inch on a short trip to a garage — 10 lb at speed.

Refer to car handbook for correct tyre pressures, which must be increased by specified amounts when vehicle is heavily laden, towing or travelling at sustained high speeds. If using other tyres check tyre manufacturer's specifications.

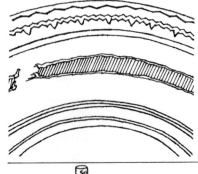

Constant rubbing of the tyres against kerbs causes serious sidewall damage which reduces the life of the tyres; look also for cuts and cracks in the tread and sidewalls.

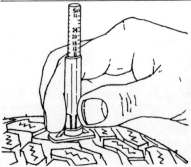

The law says the tread must be at least 1 mm deep across three-quarters of the width of the tyre and all the way round it; the AA says 2 mm is minimal for safety; you can check with a tread-depth gauge.

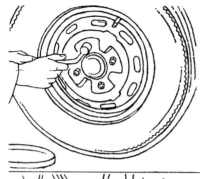

DEALING WITH FLAT TYRES

Before changing a wheel move as far off the road as possible on to flat ground; always chock the wheels. Remove hub cap and loosen nuts with wheelbrace before jacking the car up. Place nuts in hub cap.

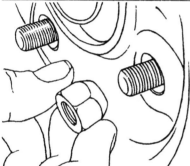

Position the spare wheel on the studs and do up the nuts finger tight. Tighten nuts progressively, working from the first nut to the one opposite. Lower car, then tighten nuts fully.

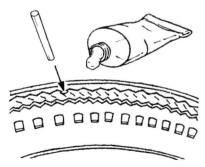

Tubeless tyres can be repaired quickly but temporarily without removing tyre from wheel by inserting a plug with a chemical solution. This repair lasts only for 100 miles at 40mph maximum. A garage will do it in a few minutes.

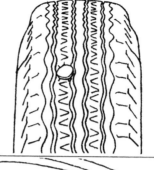

Permanent repairs require a rubber plug to be bonded into the tyre either by the use of chemicals or by heat, normally done by a garage or tyre shop; the inside of the tyre must be inspected for damage.

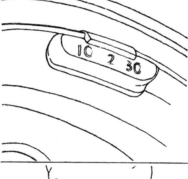

Wheel balance can be affected, causing vibration at certain speeds, when new or repaired tyres are fitted. Checking must be carried out by a garage and the wheel rebalanced with lead weights.

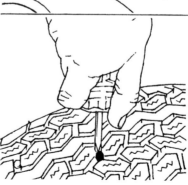

Tyre life is increased considerably if flints and stones are removed from between the treads at weekly intervals; use a screwdriver to work them out and take the opportunity to look for cuts.

TYRES

A car's contact with the road is not much greater than that of two pairs of shoes. But the tyres of a car must withstand all the dynamic stresses of a ton or more of metal hurtling around a bend at high speed.

Grip is provided by the tread. In heavy rain the zigzag grooves serve to drain the surface water to the rear of the tyre. If the road water is the thickness of a penny the tyre must move 2 gallons of water a second when the car is travelling at 60 mph.

A set of tyres should last about 20 000 miles. Wear increases dramatically if corners are taken too fast or the car is driven 'hard' with sharp acceleration and harsh braking. Because of wheel-balance problems, the popular practice of changing wheels around to prolong tyre wear is now seldom advised.

Stiff fines and a licence endorsement are the penalties of using worn or damaged tyres. Also, your insurance company may not meet an accident claim. According to the law, tyres must be

△ Free of defects and suitable for the use to which they are being put.
△ Correctly inflated.
△ Treaded to a depth of at least 1 mm across three-quarters of the width and all the way round.

Defects include cuts or tears more than an inch long in any part of the tyre, lumps or bulges, or tyres so worn that the ply is exposed.

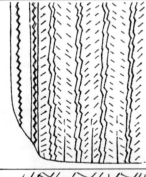

CROSSPLY

This is the conventional tyre fitted to most family saloons. Tyres which are 'remoulded' should be marked as such but sometimes are not and can easily be mistaken for new.

RADIAL

Increasingly popular, especially for faster cars, this tyre is dearer but lasts longer and has better grip, especially on corners. Its softness often gives the impression that it is deflating.

TYRE MARKINGS

There is no standard tyre marking. Tyres don't have to be marked with anything. The marking opposite is typical, but marks do vary a lot. Some sizes are measured in millimetres.

R   6PR   5.20 – 12   SR   1020 lb
    Ply rating (indication of strength)
Radial   Width of tread in inches
        Diameter of rim in inches
        Maximum speed rating (113 mph)
        Maximum load rating

SPEED LIMITS

Few people know that tyres must be run in (do not exceed 50 mph or corner fast for first 100 miles) or that tyres have a speed limit. Remoulds or retreads should not exceed 70 mph on a 10-in wheel, 75 mph on a larger wheel. The following are the coded speed limits of tyres.

		RIM DIAMETER		
		10 in	12 in	13 in-plus
CROSSPLY	No mark	75 mph	85 mph	95 mph
	S	97 mph	100 mph	110 mph
	H	110 mph	115 mph	125 mph
	V	110+ mph	115+ mph	125+ mph
RADIAL	SR	113 mph	113 mph	113 mph
	HR and VR	Very high speeds		
WINTER RADIAL	SR	100 mph	100 mph	100 mph

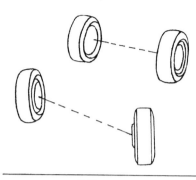

GUARDING AGAINST TYRE TROUBLE

Tyres on the same axle must by law be of the same type. If radial and cross-ply tyres must be mixed at all, NEVER fit the radials to the front as it affects braking: cross-plies on the front, radials on the rear.

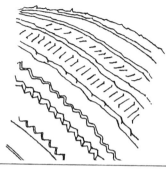

A sure sign of wheels that are out of alignment: have the car checked by a garage as soon as possible.

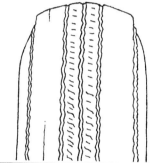

Wear on either side of the tread is caused by consistent under-inflation of the tyre, which not only wears out the rubber but increases petrol consumption and is dangerous.

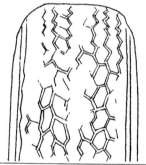

Tyre-wear in particular spots is usually caused by imbalance of the wheel or heavy braking; have the wheel balanced by a garage.

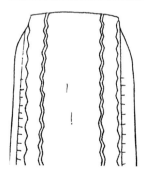

Wear in the centre of the tread is caused by too much air pressure; grip of the tread on the road is dangerously reduced.

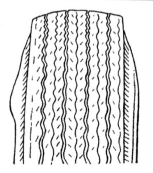

Check for this type of wear by jacking up the car and spinning each wheel, then 'sighting' along it. Bulges and lumps are caused by weak walls. The tyre must immediately be replaced.

PETROL

The routine of filling a car with petrol is familiar to every driver. But how the petrol gets from the tank to the carburettor, and how it makes the engine turn, is for many people something of a mystery. In fact, it is perfectly simple. The petrol flows through pipes which must be air tight and in good condition.

As the tank is lower than the engine, it must be pumped by a small electrical or mechanical fuel pump, which also must be clean and in good condition. The carburettor mixes the petrol with the right proportion of air, depending on whether the car is starting from cold, cruising or accelerating, and the mixture is then sucked into the cylinders where it is ignited. The carburettor is a precision instrument, with one or more fine nozzles through which the petrol is drawn, so it must be clinically clean and delicately adjusted.

It is important to use only the blend of petrol recommended in the car handbook. Additives to petrol mixed in during refining help prevent 'knocking' — detonation of only part of the mixture rather than an even combustion — but the amount of additive required depends on the type of engine. A 'low octane' petrol is cheaper and is used for less exacting or low-compression engines, while a 'high octane' petrol is used for high-performance engines. Using a lower octane than is strictly necessary can cause damage, while a high octane simply wastes money.

For simplification the octane number of petrol is rated by stars.

* *	90	* * * *	97
* * *	94	* * * * *	100

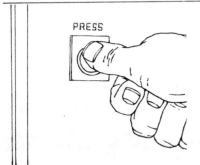

SERVING YOURSELF
The number of self-service petrol stations is growing day by day. Stop the car close to the pump, switch off and put out cigarettes. Press button to alert the attendant.

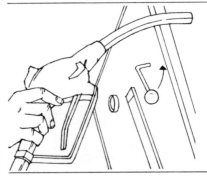

Remove nozzle from the holster, keeping it end-upwards so petrol doesn't dribble on to your clothes, switch on using the indicated lever, then insert nozzle into filler pipe of the car.

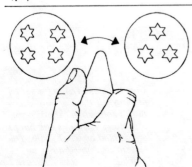

Select the star-rating to suit your car by turning the knob or indicator handle on the side of the pump. If your choice is unavailable it is better to use a higher rather than a lower octane.

Squeeze the trigger so petrol squirts into the pipe. If it suddenly stops you are filling the tank too fast, or it is nearly full. Remember to check oil, water and windscreen washer.

MASTERING THE CHOKE

To fire the engine normally requires a mixture of fifteen parts of air to one part of petrol. When the engine is cold the petrol does not vaporise so easily and a much stronger mixture – of nearly equal proportions of petrol and air – is required.

The choke acts like a strangler which reduces the air supply to the engine. As soon as the engine fires it begins to warm up, the petrol vaporises more easily, and immediately much less choke is required. By reducing the amount of choke the driver allows more air to mix with the petrol.

If the choke is used excessively too much petrol is sucked into the engine. Apart from being wasteful, this washes oil off the sides of the cylinders causing unnecessary wear, and the petrol dilutes the oil.

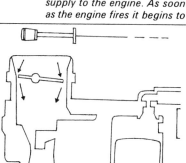

The choke control on the car's dashboard operates a flap in the air-intake of the carburettor. When the knob is pulled out the flap closes, restricting the amount of air that can be sucked through.

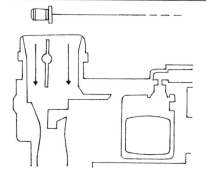

When the choke control is pushed home the flap permits a free flow of air into the carburettor. Some cars have an automatic choke set by fully depressing the accelerator pedal before starting the engine (see handbook).

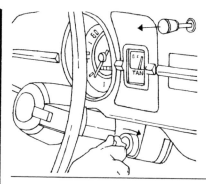

COLD-STARTING ROUTINE

Pull out choke to full extent (or fully depress and release accelerator pedal if choke is automatic). Start engine with only a little use of accelerator, if any. Reduce choke immediately until engine runs sweetly.

Immediately move away, using modest acceleration and driving gently; reduce choke as soon as possible. At traffic lights or any other delay use just enough choke to keep engine turning.

DO NOT:

△ Allow the engine to idle when cold.
△ Race the engine on starting to warm it.
△ Use any more choke than is necessary.
△ Use the choke at all if the engine is already warm.
△ Use the choke to get extra power.
△ Try to adjust an automatic choke – take the car to a garage.

TUNING AND MAINTAINING THE CARBURETTOR

The carburettor is the most delicate part of an engine. If it is out of adjustment fuel consumption can rise by up to 17 per cent without any noticeable difference in performance. But if properly serviced and checked at the correct intervals it should give no trouble.

The tuning of the carburettor is the fine adjustment of the jets through which petrol is drawn and mixed with air. This is done with the engine at its proper working temperature and idling.

Rough idling can also be caused by such things as tappets in need of adjustment, valves in bad condition, and leaks in the fuel system or the manifold. Therefore if no improvement can be made by adjusting the carburettor it is wise to seek expert assistance at a garage.

Other carburettor maintenance work can be carried out by do-it-yourself mechanics, but it is important to have the workshop manual for guidance. Cleanliness in this kind of work is essential, because it requires only a small speck of dirt to block a jet and cause trouble.

Do not try to be too ambitious, a carburettor is a complicated instrument. Dismantling it requires not only the assistance of large-scale drawings in the workshop manual, but also painstaking attention to the location of tiny needles, springs and washers.

The simple jobs listed on these two pages can be carried out on two of the most common types of carburettor without having to dismantle any complicated parts, and with little risk of causing damage to the machinery.

FIXED-JET CARBURETTOR (ZENITH/SOLEX TYPE)

MAINTENANCE

△ Check and lightly oil all linkages.

△ Check tightness and condition of fuel-pipe connection.

△ Check that when the choke knob is pushed right home there is a clearance of about 2 mm at the lever which moves the choke flap.

TUNING

1 Warm the engine to full operating temperature and leave it idling.

2 If necessary remove the air cleaner.

3 Adjust the throttle-stop screw so the engine idles with the ignition light only just extinguished.

4 Turn the volume-control screw one way until the engine almost stalls.

5 Counting the turns, turn the same screw the other way until the engine almost stalls.

6 Turn the screw back by half the number of turns you have made (the ideal position is halfway between one stalling point and the other).

7 Re-adjust throttle-stop screw if necessary.

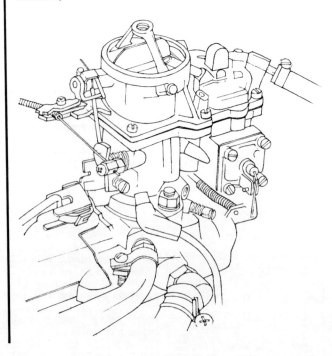

VARIABLE-JET CARBURETTOR (SU/STROMBERG TYPE)

MAINTENANCE

△ Check and lightly oil all linkages.

△ Check tightness and condition of fuel-pipe connection.

△ Check that when choke knob is pressed right home there is a 2-mm clearance at the lever which moves the choke flap.

△ When the piston-lifting pin is pressed upwards and released a sharp click indicates that the piston is returning properly.

△ Some Stromberg carburettors have two choke positions, for winter and summer; check correct one is in use.

△ Top up piston damper every 3000 miles with light oil (usually grade SAE 20 — check with handbook).

TUNING

1 Warm engine to full operating speed and leave it idling; ensure choke is not in operation.

2 If necessary remove the air cleaner.

3 Adjust the throttle-stop screw so the engine idles with the ignition light only just extinguished.

4 Raise the piston-lifting pin slightly — about $\frac{1}{32}$ in.

5 Engine revs should increase a little, then settle down.

6 If revs increase a lot and stay that way, the mixture is too rich — screw the jet-adjusting nut up a quarter of a turn and check again.

7 If revs immediately decrease, the mixture is too weak — screw the jet-adjusting nut down a quarter of a turn and check again.

8 When the right mixture is achieved adjust the throttle-stop screw again.

9 The fast-idle screw is adjusted to give a fast tickover when the choke is pulled out only a short way.

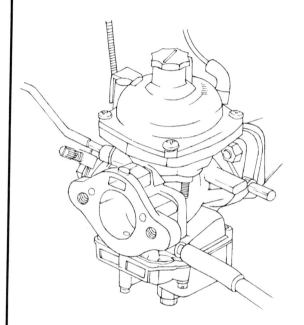

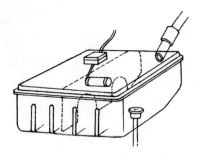

LOOKING FOR FUEL TROUBLE

If the filler cap has no small hole to let air through there is a vent tube which is prone to blockage by underseal, dirt or fluff, causing a vacuum in the tank and preventing petrol from flowing out.

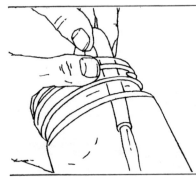

To check that fuel is reaching the carburettor disconnect the fuel pipe, direct it into a tin; operate fuel pump (by hand if mechanical, turn on ignition if electrical) and petrol should spurt out.

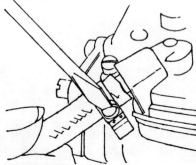

If the petrol in the container is full of bubbles look for a possible air leak between the tank and the pump; tighten and check all connections and fuel pipes.

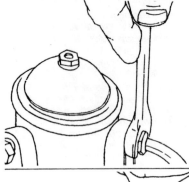

If no petrol reaches the carburettor disconnect the inlet pipe to the pump: if no petrol flows out any blockage can often be freed by blowing sharply through the pipe; also check tank vent.

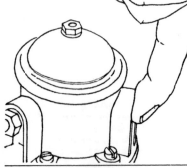

Check suction of the pump by placing finger over inlet hole and operating it. If there is no suction, blockage may be cured by blowing through the pump, or dismantling and cleaning it.

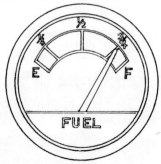

Fuel trouble can be avoided by keeping the tank topped up so sediment at the bottom is not sucked into the fuel pump and carburettor. If there is water in the petrol tank, the tank must be drained.

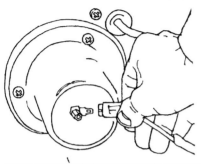

CLEANING THE FUEL PUMP

An electrical pump is situated near the tank: check electrical connections, particularly the earth; clean contacts beneath dust cap, brush filter lightly with petrol.

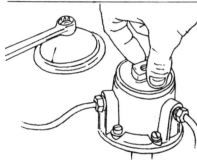

A mechanical pump, recognisable by its domed shape, is at the side of the engine: remove dome carefully; take out and clean filter in petrol, remembering which way up it goes.

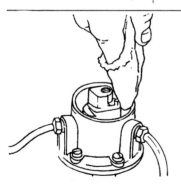

Wipe inside of pump with a clean rag. A faulty mechanical fuel pump can sometimes be restarted by a smart tap with a spanner on the body of the pump; this will dislodge any dirt in the valve seatings.

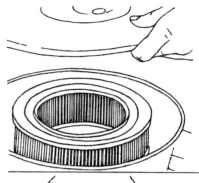

MAINTAINING THE AIR CLEANER

A paper-element filter must be replaced when it is very dirty. The top of the air cleaner is usually held only by one nut which is easily removed. Take care not to drop anything down the carburettor air intake.

A wire-mesh air filter can be removed from its housing, brushed in petrol, then dipped in oil, allowed to drain, and be replaced. This job should be done more often in dusty conditions.

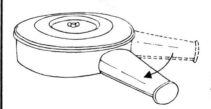

In some cars the air intake is positioned to draw in air warmed by the exhaust manifold in winter, and altered to suck in cold air in summer: follow specific directions in car handbook.

ELECTRICS

Most breakdowns are caused by ignition faults, and ignition trouble can usually be traced back to either a badly maintained battery, or dirty or faulty points or spark plugs. If battery, electrical connections, points, plug leads and spark plugs are kept in good order there should be no reason to expect trouble when starting or on the road.

Ignition problems also tend to show up when starting the car, because the system is susceptible to condensation and cold. If it takes ten seconds of starter-motor use to get the engine going the battery has to provide power equivalent to that needed for seventy headlamps. And the battery requires at least five miles of high-speed running to be recharged.

In other words, if you crawl slowly to and from the station every week-day, with wipers, headlights and radio working, the battery is never fully topped up. It pays to take the car for a good run at the weekend to recharge the battery.

A simple test of the strength in the battery can be made: face the car towards a wall, turn on the headlights and rev the engine. If the lights brighten, then dim as the engine returns to idling speed, the battery is becoming seriously weak and needs recharging.

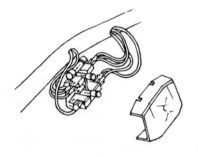

REPLACING A FUSE
A fault which overloads the car's electrical circuit will melt the fuse and break the electrical circuit. The fuse box, usually behind the fascia, contains a row of fuses wired to different circuits in the car, and also some spare ones.

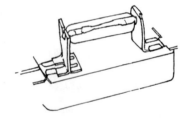

To replace a fuse press it firmly between the metal prongs. Use only a fuse with the correct rating (15, 17, 25 or 35 amps) and never use tinfoil or thick wire to effect a temporary repair.

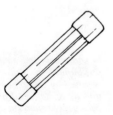

If several things fail at once – e.g. horn, wipers, interior light – suspect a blown fuse: paper inside the fuse will be charred. If a new replacement fuse also blows carefully check wiring for fault.

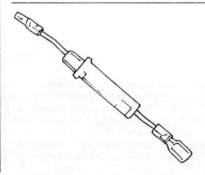

A line fuse is held between two caps which are screwed together. Check handbook for location, rating and task of all fuses, and always carry some spare ones of each rating.

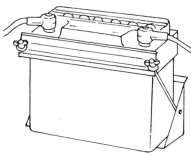

BATTERY CARE

Water in the battery should be $\frac{1}{4}$ in above the tops of the lead plates. Check it weekly, more often on long journeys and in hot weather. Ensure the car is level; do not smoke or hold a flame over the battery when charging as inflammable hydrogen gas is released.

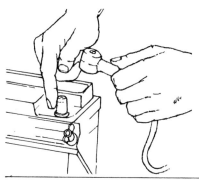

Vibration frequently causes battery connections to become loose: regularly tighten connections, clean terminals back to bare metal and smear with Vaseline, never engine grease.

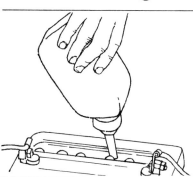

When topping up the battery use only distilled water. Follow precise instructions in car handbook. In very cold weather run the engine immediately afterwards. Dry top of battery with cloth.

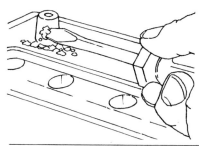

Wipe or scrape off any accumulated corrosive deposit and treat affected areas with diluted ammonia to neutralise the acid, then wash off and dry. Check battery-mounting tray for corrosion.

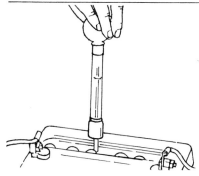

State of charge of the battery can be measured by a hydrometer, which indicates the specific gravity in the cell, normally between 1.27 and 1.29. A small amount of water is sucked up into the glass tube and a reading taken from the scale. If it is below 1.12 the battery needs charging.

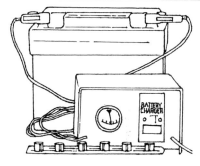

A battery not in use gradually discharges itself. Any battery can be recharged using a home charger that runs off mains electricity. Adequate ventilation is essential; any open flame is dangerous.

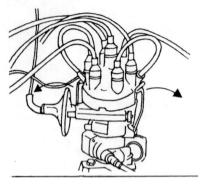

IGNITION MAINTENANCE

Turn off ignition, disconnect battery. Clean outside of distributor with petrol-damp rag, peel back weather-protection skirt (if fitted), pull aside spring clips and lift off distributor cap.

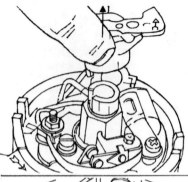

Pull off the rotor by lifting upwards; clean accumulated deposit from its metal face. Place one or two drops of any thin oil on its spindle and a touch of grease on the cam beneath it.

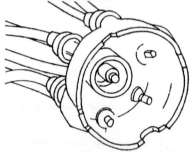

Clean inside of distributor cap with cloth; check for scratches, chips or 'tracking lines'. The latter indicate high-voltage leak: if these are found the unit must be fully checked by an expert.

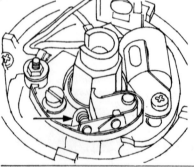

Turn the engine (by rocking the car in top gear, or by jacking up and turning the drive wheels) until the contact points are fully open.

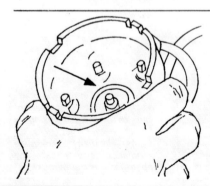

Check the central carbon brush, which is spring loaded to keep it in constant contact with the rotor; scrape with the end of screwdriver any accumulated deposit from the electrodes inside the cap.

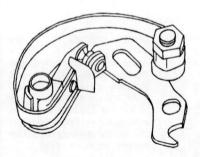

Contact points ought to be renewed if they are pitted, but can be rubbed clean with a fine file as a temporary measure. Some sets can be replaced in one piece (check your handbook), to make the fiddly job much easier.

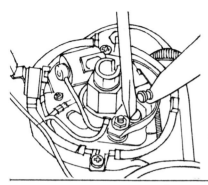

Contacts must be re-set to the correct width after maintenance. This is done by slackening the adjusting screw and using the correct feeler gauge to set the exact gap: refer to car handbook.

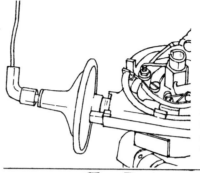

The vacuum-control, which is connected to the carburettor by a thin pipe and advances the spark as load on the engine increases, is checked by turning the whole assembly clockwise.

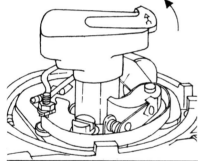

The centrifugal control, which varies the timing of the spark according to engine speed, is checked by turning the rotor anti-clockwise.

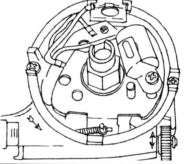

Some stiffness is felt because the assembly is spring loaded, but if it feels unduly stiff the plate beneath the contact points is in need of cleaning.

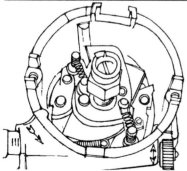

If the rotor does not return freely to its original position there is dirt obstructing the weights and springs assembled beneath the contact-points plate.

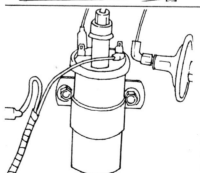

Check all connections on the coil, wipe off any dirt, clean any corrosion with sandpaper or fine file and smear with Vaseline. Refer to handbook for other ignition maintenance jobs, e.g. lubrication of generator.

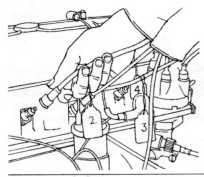

KEEPING SPARK PLUGS BRIGHT

Spark plugs must be cleaned every 3000–5000 miles and replaced every 10 000–12 000 miles. To ensure leads do not get muddled, label them or remove one at a time.

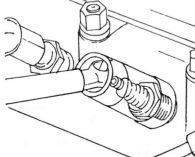

Clean each lead and look for signs of deterioration, such as insulation cracks, that could cause trouble. Use box-type spanner and bar, making sure it is properly seated, to unscrew plugs.

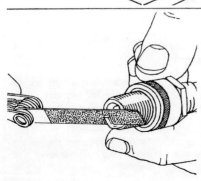

Use soft wire brush or have plugs sandblasted by a garage to remove accumulated deposit; with a small file square up the electrodes.

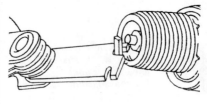

Use a plug-setting tool to bend the side electrode (never the centre one) to exactly the right gap; test with the recommended thickness of feeler gauge (refer to car handbook).

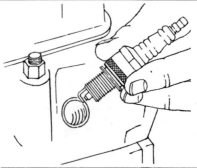

Replacing plugs: make the first few turns with the fingers to avoid crossing threads. Do not overtighten as the threads are easily stripped.

Thoroughly clean the terminal and make sure it is fitted the right way up. Clean the ceramic insulator, which causes loss of power if covered in road-dirt or grease.

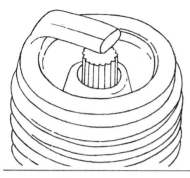

POINTERS TO TROUBLE

The condition of the spark plugs can indicate other faults in the engine. A normal plug has a light dusty brown or grey deposit with slight wear of the electrodes.

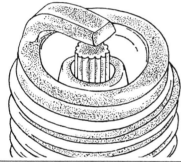

Powdery black carbon indicates too much fuel is reaching the cylinder — either the carburettor needs adjusting, the driver uses too much choke, the air-cleaner is clogged or the car is left idling too long.

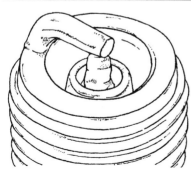

Badly eroded and pitted electrodes show the plug is getting too hot — there is a fault in the cooling system, the engine is too frequently overloaded, or octane rating of fuel is too low.

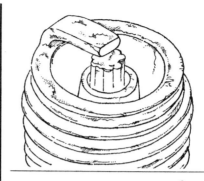

Black and liquid oily scale on the plug shows that the piston rings or valve guides have worn and oil is reaching the combustion chamber of the cylinder — an engine overhaul by a garage is indicated.

IS THE SPARK REACHING THE PLUG?

To check whether the high-voltage pulse is reaching the plugs disconnect one lead, peel back the rubber cover, hold it by the rubber lead, turn engine with ignition on.

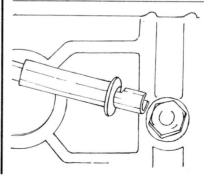

Then when the metal end of the lead is held close to a good earth (bare metal part of engine or car-body) a spark will jump across the gap: if no spark check coil and contact points.

LIGHTS

Many drivers overlook the fact that car lights have two purposes. One is to illuminate the road ahead, so the driver can see where he is going. The second, and the one most often forgotten, is to light up the car so it can *be seen* by other drivers. Sidelights are mainly only parking lights and are quite inadequate for driving, particularly when surrounded by lots of other brighter lights.

Most modern headlights are sealed-beam units in which the reflector, lens and filaments act like a single large bulb. They are more expensive to replace but much less prone to deterioration through age and moisture. In each bulb there are usually two tungsten filaments, one of 60 watts which gives a straight-ahead beam for long-distance illumination and the other of 45 watts which throws a broad and low beam that does not dazzle oncoming drivers. When one filament blows the whole unit must be replaced.

Quartz-halogen or tungsten-halogen bulbs give a brighter and more powerful light and can be used to replace ordinary bulbs of the plug-in type. Such bulbs should not be handled with bare fingers because perspiration damages the quartz; handle with a cloth or glove.

If lights flicker and work better after a hard rap with the knuckles suspect a faulty earth connection, probably caused by corrosion. Dismantle and clean the unit, and check the wiring connections.

It is not wise to tamper with wiring behind the dashboard, because many modern cars have fragile printed circuits which are easily damaged: get help from a garage.

REPLACING A HEADLAMP UNIT OR BULB

Undo the screws of the headlight trim and remove it.

Undo the retaining screws holding the unit in place, but do not alter the positioning screws.

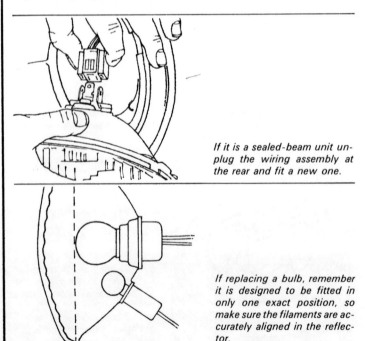

If it is a sealed-beam unit unplug the wiring assembly at the rear and fit a new one.

If replacing a bulb, remember it is designed to be fitted in only one exact position, so make sure the filaments are accurately aligned in the reflector.

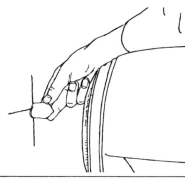

CHECKING THE ALIGNMENT OF THE HEADLAMPS

Accurate alignment of headlamps is essential and ought to be carried out by a garage. The following method, however, can be carried out at home, but it is a rough guide only. Drive the car up to a wall and mark the centre and level of each light.

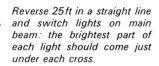

Reverse 25 ft in a straight line and switch lights on main beam: the brightest part of each light should come just under each cross.

Adjust the positioning screws behind the headlamp trim accordingly, blocking off one lamp while the other is being checked.

Alignment should be rechecked while car is towing a trailer or carrying a heavy load. Correction lenses or different bulbs should be fitted for continental motoring.

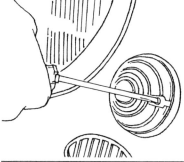

REPLACING A SMALL BULB

When a bulb fails in a tail-light cluster, indicator lamp or side-light, first unscrew the plastic lens.

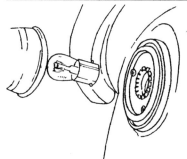

Remove failed bulb and substitute new one. If it flickers or fails to light up the electrical contacts of the light assembly are probably corroded and need cleaning with sandpaper.

UNDERBODY MAINTENANCE

The underneath of a car is constantly subjected to wetness, dirt, damage from flying stones and the corrosive effects of salt spread on the roads in winter. Yet it is here that many of the car's most important working parts – from a control and safety point of view – are located. In a short time these parts become caked with dirt which obscures any defects. Also, grit is easily worked between moving metal surfaces, hastening their wear.

The parts of the car most susceptible to this kind of damage are the steering and suspension. If they are not kept in good condition braking efficiency can be halved and tyre wear doubled, while the car is also liable to behave unpredictably and could cause an accident.

The days of greasing more than a score of nipples beneath the car every 500 miles are long gone, but the underbody of the car still requires regular and careful maintenance. Most components that required regular greasing are now sealed for life or have self-lubricating bushes. If a squeak develops add a touch of hydraulic brake fluid, not grease or oil which will attack the rubber bushes. Those nipples that do still require regular greasing (see car handbook) are often hard to find, and are easily confused with the brake-bleed points.

It is important to have the steering and suspension geometry checked by a garage every 5000–6000 miles, although by keeping it in good order yourself this should be a mere formality. While driving listen for strange knocks or rattles which can be early indicators of trouble before it gets too serious. Do not tamper with Hydrolastic, Hydrogas or Hydropneumatique suspensions, which require special equipment and expert attention.

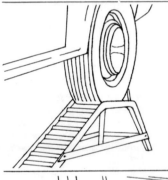

WORKING UNDER THE CAR
Never work under a car which is held up only by a jack, or by bricks or tins which could easily collapse. Either use a pair of wheel ramps to raise one end of the car.

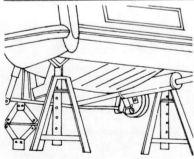

Or jack the car up and lower it on to a pair of stands; solid baulks of timber can also be used. If the front of the car is raised apply the handbrake firmly; if the rear is raised firmly chock the front wheels.

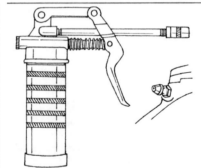

USING A GREASE-GUN
A grease-gun is used to squirt grease under high pressure into the small nozzles called nipples. First clean the nipple and ensure it is not blocked; use the recommended type of grease.

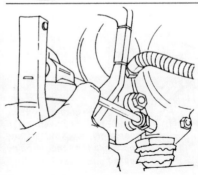

Put nozzle of grease-gun over nipple and pump grease into it until old grease is seen spurting out of joints.

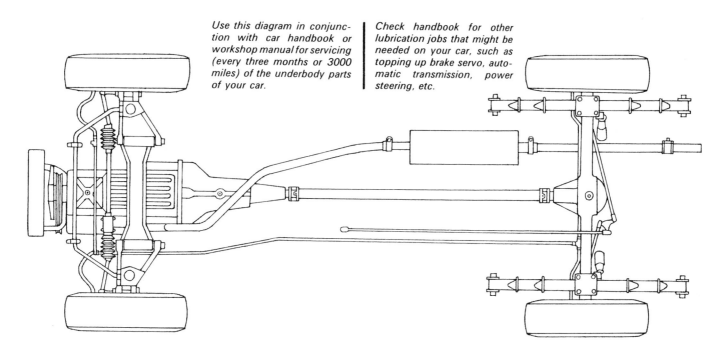

Use this diagram in conjunction with car handbook or workshop manual for servicing (every three months or 3000 miles) of the underbody parts of your car.

Check handbook for other lubrication jobs that might be needed on your car, such as topping up brake servo, automatic transmission, power steering, etc.

TRUNNIONS
Check for wear.

BALL JOINTS
Check for wear.

MOUNTING OF ANTI-ROLL BAR
Check for wear, tightness.

TIE-ROD CONNECTING POINT
Check for wear, tightness.

RUBBER BUMP-STOP
Check for damage.

LEAF-SPRINGS
Check for damage, especially at mounting points; clean with wire brush.

U-BOLTS
Check tightness.

PROPELLER-SHAFT COUPLINGS
Check tightness of bolts.

RUBBER BOOTS AND GAITERS
Check for splits that will allow grease and oil to spill out and grit to enter.

HYDRAULIC SUSPENSION DAMPERS (SHOCK ABSORBERS)
Check for oil leaks.

STEERING
Check tightness of bolts holding steering box or rack-and-pinion steering gear to chassis.

KING-PINS
Check for wear by jacking up car and rocking wheel with footbrake applied.

HINGES (doors, bonnet, boot)
Oil regularly.

GREASE NIPPLES
Likely to be fitted to steering swivels, ball joints, handbrake and clutch cables, propeller shaft, universal joints, suspension shackles.

CHECKING BRAKES

Regular maintenance of the braking system is essential to safety. Some checks can be made while you are driving, but often deterioration is quite slow and you may not notice that the brakes are getting bad. They should be checked every 6000 miles or six-monthly, including the handbrake.

Braking systems vary considerably, so follow exactly the adjustment and checking procedures described in the car handbook. For safety, if doubtful about your ability to do a maintenance job seek expert assistance.

Trouble often shows up in the 'feel' of the brake pedal. If the pedal travels more than one-third of its possible distance before the brakes come on hard the system needs adjustment. A spongy feel to the brakes indicates there is air in the hydraulic system: the fluid must be drained and the system bled and topped up. If the braking still feels spongy the whole system must be thoroughly checked for air leaks. The need to top up the master cylinder also points to trouble: there is a leak in the system and it must be traced at once by a garage or failure could occur at any moment.

Efficiency of the brake pads and linings depends on their ability to absorb heat as well as friction, so running them down to the last fraction of wear is a short-sighted policy. Because of the increased strain on the brakes, they should be relined if they are more than half worn out before a holiday in which a boat-trailer or caravan is being towed.

When testing brakes on the road first check that tyre pressures are correct. Any tendency to pull to one side could be corrected by adjustment of the brakes. If you are still doubtful take the car to a garage. All rubber seals and brake hoses in the hydraulic system should be replaced after about three years or 40 000 miles.

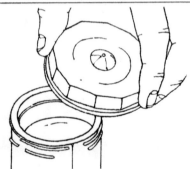

TOPPING UP THE MASTER CYLINDER
The reservoir of hydraulic brake fluid must be checked weekly. Clean the cap and area around it before removing it. Check level and clear vent hole in cap. Use only approved brake fluid.

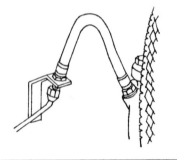

CHECKING BRAKE HOSES
Hoses and pipes carrying brake fluid under pressure to the brakes are prone to corrosion from salt and damage from stones: check hoses for fraying, stretching, cuts or general deterioration.

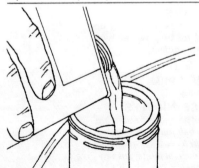

Top up with new brake fluid. Avoid shaking up the can. Do not store fluid in an open or partly filled can. Do not spill on paint. Replace fluid every eighteen months or 15 000 miles.

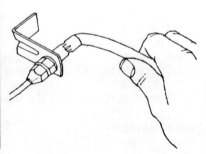

Couplings in the hydraulic system must also be checked for damage, tightness and wear: any sign of seepage of fluid must be dealt with immediately.

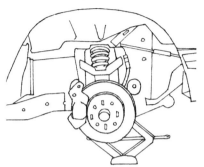

CHECKING DISC BRAKES

Disc brakes are usually fitted only to the front wheels. Jack the car up and remove front wheel. Put handbrake on.

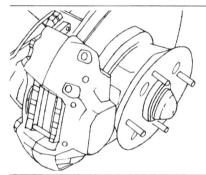

Disc brakes are normally self-adjusting, but it is important to check how much wear remains in the pads.

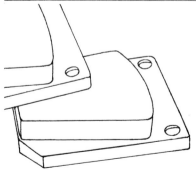

Brake pads should not be allowed to wear down to less than one-third of their original thickness, or less than $\frac{1}{8}$ in thickness. Replacement of pads is easily done with guidance of a workshop manual.

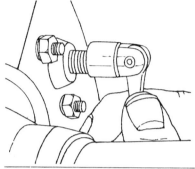

CHECKING AND ADJUSTING DRUM BRAKES

The square adjusting nut is on the inside of the brake back-plate; front drum brakes may have two nuts. Secure the other wheel, jack up and spin the wheel. Tighten nut until wheel stops, then release so wheel is just free.

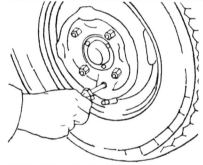

Some drum brakes are adjusted by inserting a screw-driver through a hole in the drum and turning a screw. Use the same method indicated above. Make sure handbrake is in 'off' position.

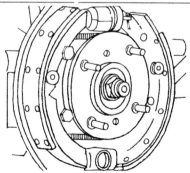

To check brake shoes remove wheel; slacken brake adjusters; remove brake drum. Clean dust out of the drum and inspect for wear. Check that the linings have not worn down to the level of the rivets. Do not leave oily stains on the linings.

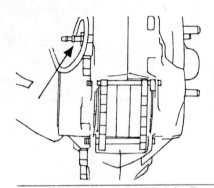

BLEEDING THE BRAKES

When air enters the hydraulic system the brakes must be bled to get rid of it. Top up the master cylinder. Start with the brake furthest away from it. Clean the brake-bleed nipple thoroughly.

Continue until the fluid draining out of the nipple into the jar is clean and clear of bubbles. Make sure the master cylinder is continually topped up to at least the midway mark.

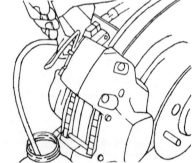

Use a clean plastic or rubber hose about 18 in long which is a close fit over the nipple. Direct end into a jar so it is immersed in new brake fluid. With a spanner release nipple one turn.

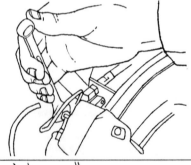

With the brake pedal fully depressed tighten the bleed nipple firmly (but not too much) and remove the hose.

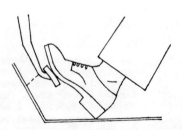

Helper sitting in driving seat should then pump the brake pedal right to the floor, allow it to return, slowly, then repeat several times.

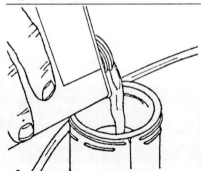

Top up master cylinder with fresh brake fluid and repeat with the next brake concluding with that nearest to the master cylinder. If brakes still feel spongy seek expert attention.

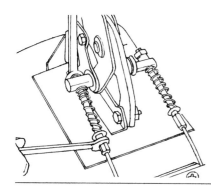

ADJUSTING THE HANDBRAKE

Before adjusting rear brakes note travel of handbrake lever. After adjustment take up any slack in the cable by turning and adjusting nuts, found under the carpet or under the car.

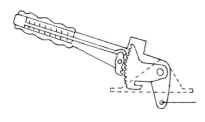

When the handbrake is hard on it should be positioned one-third of the way up its travel. Then jack up the car to check that the wheels are free to rotate when the handbrake is released. Check for frayed cables and linkages and replace if necessary.

CLUTCH

Most modern cars have hydraulic clutch release mechanisms which are usually self-adjusting or simple cable systems. Little maintenance is required until the clutch plate has to be relined. This job is best done by a garage. Wear is considerably increased by drivers who rest their left foot on the pedal while the engine is going and who hold the car stationary on a hill by deliberately 'slipping' the clutch to save using the handbrake.

The master cylinder of cars with a hydraulic clutch must be topped up in the same way, with the same precautions, as the brake master cylinder.

The clutch pedal should have about 1 in of free play before the clutch begins to disengage. A juddering clutch indicates wear or need for adjustment; a slipping clutch indicates oil on the plates.

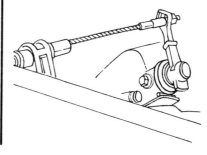

If the clutch is mechanical, regularly oil all linkages and adjust by taking up on the adjusting nut, the position of which is detailed in the car handbook.

EXHAUST AND SILENCER

The gases which are the residue of combustion in the cylinders are pushed into the exhaust manifold of the engine by the first upward stroke of the piston. The manifold directs the gases into the exhaust pipe, which carries them to the rear of the car where they escape into the air. Near the end of the exhaust pipe is a silencer, comprising sound-insulating material or baffles, which cut down the noise. Drivers are required by law to ensure that their engines are running quietly.

The exhaust and silencer are particularly liable to rust: partly because they are under the body of the car, where they bear the brunt of salt and flying stones; and partly because condensation collects inside the exhaust pipe, causing it to rust from within.

The system must be kept in good condition because lethal exhaust gases can leak unnoticed through a tiny pinhole in the metal and seep into the passenger compartment of the car.

Few exhaust pipes and silencers last more than about two winters before they must be replaced. If part of the pipe or one of the supporting straps breaks it is advisable to replace the whole thing, as it is all made of thin metal which tends to corrode at the same rate. Recently, stainless steel systems have overcome this defect but are available only from specialist firms.

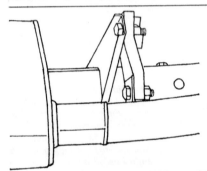

Check supporting straps. To prevent vibration they are made of rubber-and-webbing collars, thick rubber loops, or rubber-mounted metal bands, all of which are prone to deterioration.

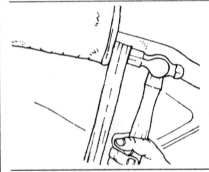

When removing an old system for replacement first soak joints in penetrating oil, then free them with light hammering and by twisting the pipe. Install the new pipe from the front end, working back.

Ensure that all joints are tight, and inspect the top of the pipe, as well as the bottom, for corrosion. Pin-hole leaks are practically impossible to detect, so replace a pipe that is badly pitted or damaged.

Condition of the exhaust smoke can indicate engine trouble: blue smoke shows that oil is entering the cylinders; black soot in the pipe shows the mixture is too rich; white deposits show the mixture is too weak.

WINDSCREEN WIPERS AND WASHER

The windscreen wipers are driven by an electric motor, which is a sealed unit and seldom needs attention. If the wipers fail, find the correct fuse, using the wiring diagram in the handbook, then check it and the connections to the motor and wiper switch.

The usual trouble is progressive deterioration which passes unnoticed until very bad conditions occur and the wipers simply cannot cope with all the rain and road-water.

The wiper blades are made of soft rubber which remains in good condition for only about a year and needs to be replaced.

The windscreen washer needs to be topped up weekly. Do not add anti-freeze to the water as this will corrode the plastic or rubber tubes. To prevent windscreen smear do not add household detergent, which makes the problem worse, but add a spoonful of ammonia or a proprietary windscreen-wash additive.

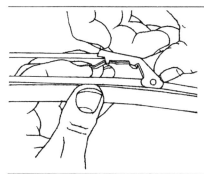

New windscreen-wiper blades should be fitted every autumn. Most types are removed from the wiper arm with a strong, even pull, though some are screwed or held by spring clips.

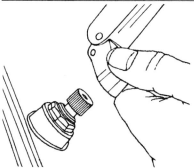

If the wipers do not park correctly they can be repositioned by pulling the entire arm off the drive spindle – it is usually held by a small clip or spring – and pressing it back in a new position.

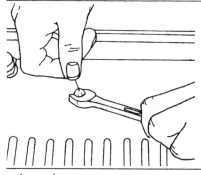

The windscreen-washer nozzles can be adjusted with a pin or thin wire. The jets of water should be aimed high so that the slipstream of the car at speed will deflect them down on to the glass.

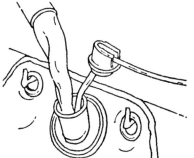

Check connections of the plastic tubes of the washer unit every three months, for they can easily become pinched and restrict supply, or chafe through. The reservoir can be filled with clean tap water.

CAR-BODY CARE

Clean water, and lots of it, is all that is needed for washing the car. It helps a little if the water is tepid. Car shampoos do not seem to help much – just a drop of detergent (thick suds are not necessary) or a spoonful of paraffin can be added to the washing water to help remove traffic film.

Regular cleaning, once every week or fortnight, is important if the appearance of the car is to be preserved and its re-sale value maintained. The enemies of car paint are bird droppings (particularly seagulls'), fruit and berry juices, lime trees, sea spray, salted roads and industrial fallout such as cement dust or invisible chemicals. Unless these are removed from the paint immediately, corrosion begins at once.

Cleaning also gives you the chance to spot scratches in the paint before they become rusty patches; small scars can be touched up quickly.

The value of polishing has been questioned by organisations such as the AA, which has carried out extensive tests. Although polishing does to some extent improve appearance, particularly of an old car, regular washing with clean water is thought to be just as good.

CLEANING THE CAR
Starting from the horizontal surfaces, then working round the car, sponge away accumulated dirt, using plenty of cold or tepid water and regularly rinsing the sponge to remove grit.

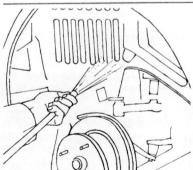

Remove caked dirt and salt from beneath car and inaccessible areas of wings, using a powerful hose. Do not squirt water on to windows as their waterproofing seals are not strong enough.

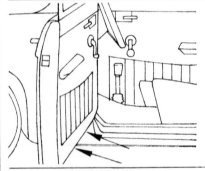

Beneath each door there are drain holes which must be cleaned out with thin wire; refer to car handbook for exact location of these and other holes; clean jacking point and insides of bumpers.

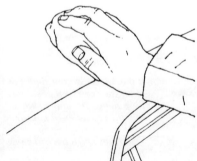

Dry off the surface water with a soft chamois leather rinsed out frequently. This rubbing does the car as much good as polishing. Water stains will remain if the sun is very bright.

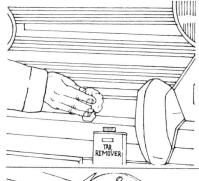

Spots of tar accumulated on the front areas of the car and near the wings can be removed with a soft cloth soaked in white spirit, turpentine or tar-remover.

Blemishes on the chrome trim should be cleaned with chrome-cleaner and given a good rub. Aluminium and stainless steel brightwork needs only a wash and a rub. Do not use metal polish.

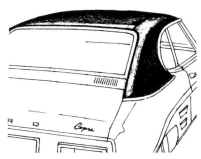

Warm water and toilet soap, or upholstery cleaner, should be used on a leather-cloth roof. Do not use detergent, car shampoo or household soap.

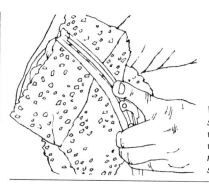

Windscreen-wiper blades should be cleaned carefully with methylated spirits or wiped with a sponge reserved for the purpose; detergent will smear the glass.

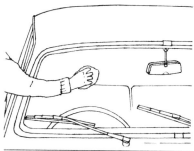

Warm water removes squashed insects and other stains from the windscreen and windows. Allow glass to dry, then clean with domestic window cleaner. Never use paint or metal polish on glass.

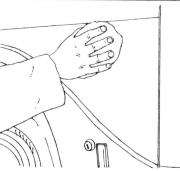

To brighten dull paintwork a mild rubbing-down compound may prove more lasting than car polish: apply with a soft cloth and follow maker's instructions after checking that it is suitable for your car.

TOUCHING UP PAINTWORK

Wear and tear on bodywork inevitably damages small areas of paintwork which, if not attended to immediately, will erupt into spots of rust which will spread and blemish the appearance of the car as well as weaken the body panels. The damage is caused by flying flints and stones, and the doors of other cars hitting the side of your car when they are opened.

Rust is fairly easily dealt with in its early stages, but after as little time as a fortnight can be so well established that removal is a major job.

The most serious type of body corrosion starts from beneath the paint, usually from inside the metal frame of the basic structure, and is not caused only by dampness or exposure to the air. Many things contribute to corrosion, including the way the metal faces are treated during manufacture, electrolytic action, and condensation. In the exhaust pipe and silencer, for example, corrosion is hastened by acids in the exhaust gases which attack the pipe from the inside.

DEALING WITH PAINT CHIPS
A small tin of touch-up paint to match the colour of the car should be kept in the garage so it can be applied to small paint chips as they occur. Follow the maker's instructions.

Remove any rust by rubbing with 'wet-and-dry' emery paper (fine grade) until all traces have been removed and only bright metal can be seen. Apply a dab of rust neutraliser.

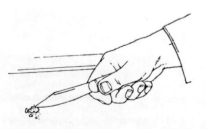

Remove any flaking paint from the affected area and wash thoroughly with white spirit and soft cloth to remove any old polish which will prevent the paint from sticking.

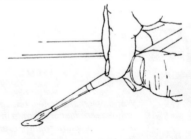

Small new chips may require only one tiny spot of paint, but larger areas should be given one coat of primer, then, when that is dry and rubbed down, a coat of coloured paint. Protect the wet paint from dust. Don't paint on a windy day.

When the paint is thoroughly dry (it does no harm to leave it a week) gently apply rubbing-down compound to smooth it off, then wash and dry.

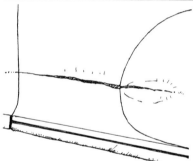

FILLING A SCRATCH

Remove any rust, using a rust-removal compound if necessary. Allow it to dry, then clean off according to maker's instructions. Lift off any flaking paint.

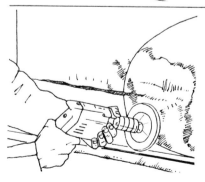

Using wet-and-dry emery paper by hand, or a disc fitted to an electric drill, sand down the area until smooth and bright; ensure that all rust and old paint are removed from the crevices.

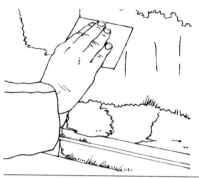

Mix filler compound as directed by maker, taking care to achieve the right consistency of paste. Press it into the scratch, using a piece of card or plastic as a trowel.

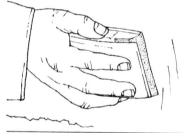

When dry, sand the filling compound smooth, using emery paper wrapped around a wooden or rubber sanding block. Mask the area to be painted with tape and news-paper.

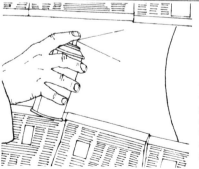

Using aerosol-type paints, apply at least two thin coats of primer and allow to dry, rubbing down after each coat, and two thin coats of colour. Do not polish top-coat for at least three months.

GOOD HOUSEKEEPING

Maintaining a car in a clean, tidy and good condition will help to keep up its value and promote careful driving. An untidy car indicates a driver who would probably be equally casual about car maintenance and safety.

Full ashtrays, dirt-engrained carpets and upholstery embedded with crumbs and other dirt soon give the inside of a car a stale smell which other people notice — particularly those interested in buying the car — even if you do not.

Tobacco smoke stains the roof lining and in little more than a week covers the inside of the windscreen and other windows with a film of tar and nicotine. This encourages mist to form on the windows because the deposit acts as nuclei for droplets of moisture to form.

The windscreen mists up on cold mornings partly because the driver's warm breath condenses on the cold glass, and also because damp air that has been lying in heater pipes since the car was last used is blown into the warm car.

Misting can be cleared most quickly by directing as much air on to it as possible, by turning up the heater full blast and directing the jet of air through the windscreen vents, and by opening the side windows. Adjustable ventilators can direct air on to the side windows so visibility is not restricted.

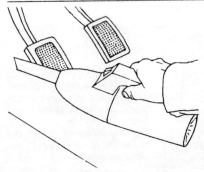

Thoroughly clean floor carpets with a stiff brush to loosen grit and dust, then remove it with a domestic vacuum-cleaner or a small battery-operated one.

Use a narrow nozzle of the vacuum-cleaner to remove grit and dirt from narrow crevices such as around the pedals, between the seats, inside the pockets, and the rear footwell.

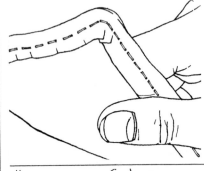

The floor-pan is frequently a rust trap because window leaks saturate underfelt and go unnoticed for months — lift all floor coverings and check for dampness; thoroughly brush out dust.

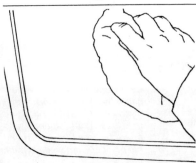

Polish the inside of all window glass regularly, not forgetting rear-vision mirrors and instrument glasses. Use ordinary domestic window cleaner applied with a soft cloth.

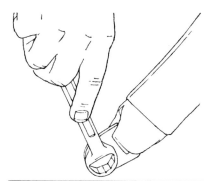

Check tightness of seatbelt attachments and ensure there are no splits or signs of fraying in the webbing. If necessary sponge webbing with warm water and a non-detergent soap.

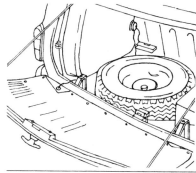

Clean out the boot; remove spare tyre and check inflation; check drain-hole in the boot is not blocked; ensure no moisture is lying in the floor-pan; oil jack and check tools.

Upholstery is cleaned with a special liquid available in motor accessory shops. It is applied with a paintbrush, then wiped away with a cloth. Do not spill the liquid on paintwork.

Any rust in the floor-pans of the passenger compartment or the boot must be thoroughly cleaned with a wire brush, then coated with rust-inhibiting paint (do not block drain-holes).

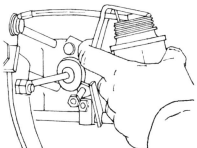

With an oil-can check and lubricate all pedal linkages; tighten steering-column bolts; oil and check seat-runners, door hinges, boot and bonnet hinges and latches, etc.

Sealing rubbers on the doors and boot lid should be checked. If coming unstuck they can be re-fixed, using sticking compound available with a squirt-nozzle. Close door until dry.

77

FIT-IT-YOURSELF ACCESSORIES

WING MIRROR
Helps to increase rearward vision and overcome blind spots and must be fitted to estate cars and cars towing, can be fitted with electric drill and a small bit.

FIRE EXTINGUISHER
It is best to fit one that is approved by the British Standards Institution. Aerosol types are not approved, though some work effectively.

CHILD SAFETY SEAT OR HARNESS
Buy only those which are approved by the British Standards Institution. Different kits are available for different models and types of car.

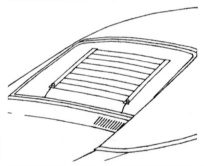

REAR-WINDOW HEATING PANEL
Melts ice and snow and evaporates mist that accumulates on rear window. Uses a lot of current and should never be left switched on.

HEADREST
Fits easily over the backrest of the seat, but ensure that the firm part of the head-pad comes up as high as the level of the eyes.

ANTI-DAZZLE MIRROR
Can be adjusted with a flick to prevent headlights of following vehicles from dazzling the driver's eyes, yet provides full rearward visibility.

FOG- AND SPOT-LAMPS

Fitted to the front of the car they are a boon for driving in fog. Extra-strong red lights for the rear of the car can also be fitted to lessen the risk of a rear-end accident in fog.

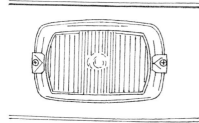

REVERSING LIGHT

Can be fitted (to modern cars only) so it automatically lights up, casting a low and wide beam to the rear of the car, when reverse gear is selected.

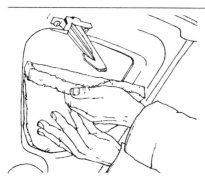

SOUND INSULATION KIT

Pre-cut pieces of thick felt are glued to inside panels, wheel arches, bonnet, boot and floor-pan to cut down on engine noise and to absorb vibration.

DOG RESTRAINT

Easily fitted to an estate car without tools being required, it prevents dogs from roaming around the car distracting the driver.

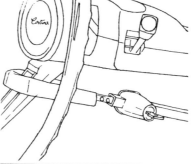

ANTI-THEFT KITS

The serious car thief will be deterred by few of the different types of immobilisers on the market, but joy-riders will be put off the idea and look for another car.

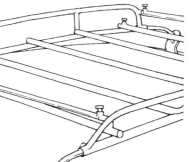

ROOFRACK

Firmly fixed to roof of car for carrying extra luggage, it should be quickly removed when not required because extra wind resistance causes drag which makes the car use more petrol.

PART IV
DON'T PANIC!

GUIDE TO SIMPLE DO-IT-YOURSELF EMERGENCY ROADSIDE REPAIRS

Sudden serious breakdown is comparatively rare in modern cars. Most trouble on the road is caused by small things, such as damp ignition or fuel blockages, which can usually be traced and dealt with on the spot.

Preventing them is easy enough. All you have to do is service the car properly and regularly according to instructions in the handbook. Trouble is invited only when servicing is skimped.

If the worst happens and the car does let you down on the road, these pages are a simple guide to getting the car going again. If you fail to get started the trouble is probably serious and it is necessary to get expert help.

IF THE BATTERY IS FLAT . . .

The unwelcome groaning sound of a starter labouring because the battery is flat is well known. There is no point in continuing if the starter gets slower and slower. It is better to save what little power there is in the battery and start the car by other means.

The trouble is sometimes caused by faulty battery connections restricting the flow of current. Clean the terminals (see p. 57) and also check the terminals of the earth strap which makes a connection between the engine and the car chassis (for location see car handbook).

PUSH START

Unless it has an automatic gear-box the car can be push-started from a brisk walking pace if you can find enough willing helpers. Ensure that your pushers are not put at risk if the road is busy. Always sit in the driving seat while the car is being pushed, don't be tempted to get out and help. When the car has reached maximum speed switch on ignition, pull out choke if engine is cold, slip into second or third gear, and release clutch slowly.

As the engine fires depress clutch again and increase revs as the car coasts to a stop. Do not try to start the car by pushing it in reverse gear.

DOWNHILL START

If battery trouble is suspected always try to leave the car pointing down a hill, because this is the easiest way of starting the engine without help from the battery.

Let the car coast down the hill, gaining momentum. Switch on ignition; pull out choke if engine is cold. Select a gear appropriate to the speed of the car (second gear and a speed of about 10 mph is ideal), then release clutch so the engine turns.

As the engine fires depress clutch, increase revs, then pull into the kerb and ensure engine is running smoothly (if this check is not made the engine might cut out again when you reach the bottom of the hill).

TOW START

Before accepting a tow from another car it is important to inform the other driver what speed you require and agree what signals you will give (one toot on the horn can indicate that you want to stop, two toots that you want to keep going or increase speed).

The tow-rope should be about 15 ft long, marked in the middle with a distinctive rag, and you should have the words 'on tow' on the rear of the car.

Attach the tow-rope only to a firm part of the car structure (see handbook), not the bumper, grille or any part of the steering. The towing vehicle should take up the slack, then move off very slowly. Keep a watch for signals indicating that the towing vehicle is having to slow down or turn. Remember that until the ignition is switched on your car will have no brake or indicator lights.

Select a gear appropriate to the speed of the car, switch on ignition and use choke if necessary, then release clutch. As engine fires depress clutch, change into neutral and signal towing vehicle to pull in.

USING TORCH BATTERIES

If the battery is so flat that it won't provide sufficient spark for starting by rolling the car, power can be supplied by torch batteries.

The total voltage of all the batteries used must equal the voltage of the car battery (if the car battery is 12 volts use two 6-volt cells, or four 3-volt cells.

They must be connected up in series, positive (+) terminal to negative (−) terminal, using wire and insulation tape.

The negative (−) terminal of the series of batteries is earthed to a bare metal part of the car, the positive (+) terminal is connected with the 'SW' lead of the coil, or vice versa if the car is 'positive-earthed'.

JUMP LEADS

Carrying a pair of jump leads in the boot means you can tap starting power from the batteries of other cars and also be in a position to offer assistance to others.

Jump leads are thick insulated cables with a clip at either end. Position the other car nearby. Join the positive (+) terminals of each battery with the red lead, and the negative terminals (−) with the black lead. It is essential that the correct terminals are connected.

The car can then be started in the normal way.

STARTER MOTOR TURNS BUT . . .

If engine does not fire, first check petrol gauge, then:

IN DAMP WEATHER

Cold air acting on an engine after it has been switched off, particularly in foggy or humid weather, can cause condensation which is the most likely cause of ignition trouble (p. 58).

1 Dry plug leads thoroughly.
2 Dry spark-plug insulators (one at a time so leads don't get muddled).
3 Dry distributor cap, all wires and top of coil.
4 Remove distributor cap and dry the inside of it.
5 Dry rotor arm.
6 Check all ignition connections.
7 Lightly spray distributor, leads and plugs with water-repellent aerosol (available at garages and accessory shops).

FOLLOW THE SPARK

1 Check that the ignition spark is reaching the spark plug (p. 61).
   If YES check fuel (see next column).
   If NO:
2 Check and clean connections on coil.
3 Clean wires and distributor; feel the wires closely for any signs of fraying or breakage beneath the insulation covering.
4 Check distributor (p. 58).
   Look for: Dirty contacts.
            Broken contacts spring.
            Dampness.
            Dirty rotor arm.

FOLLOW THE FUEL

1 Check that fuel is reaching the carburettor (p. 54).
   If YES, and spark is also present, remove spark plug for check (p. 61).
   If no fault is found the trouble is probably in the carburettor. Take to garage immediately.
   If NO:
2 Check the fuel level with a dipstick to ensure fuel gauge is not faulty.
3 If fuel is low, and car is standing on a hill or steep camber, push it on to level ground.

4 Check fuel pump (p. 55).
   If electric: Check connections.
               Sharply tap the metal part of the pump, which may clear any blockage.
   If mechanical: Clean filter.
5 Disconnect and blow through fuel lines to clear blockages.

FLOODING

The engine may exhibit symptoms of ignition failure or fuel problems when all that is wrong is flooding of the carburettor by too much petrol. This is usually caused by excessive use of the choke, especially when the engine is already warm, or excessive throttle when starting.

1 Push the choke home.
2 Depress the accelerator right down and turn the starter: this sucks excess petrol away.
3 If that doesn't work, let the engine stand for 10 to 15 minutes.

STARTER MOTOR PROBLEMS

1 If the starter does not turn check electrical connections.
2 If the starter does not turn and lights dim, it is jammed. It can be freed by turning the nut at the back of the starter (sometimes this is covered by a rubber cap).
3 If the starter whines and does not engage, the engaging gear is stuck. A sharp tap to the starter motor while it is being operated may free it.
4 If the starter labours and turns the engine slowly, check battery connections and suspect a flat battery (p. 57).

DASHBOARD WARNING LIGHTS

1 If the red ignition light does not go out when engine revs are increased check the fan-belt (p. 41) or suspect a faulty generator. The light should just flicker when the engine is idling.
2 If the green or orange oil light does not go out after a second or two switch off immediately: there is an oil-pressure fault which could seriously damage the engine. Check oil level (p. 42).

THE IGNITION SYSTEM

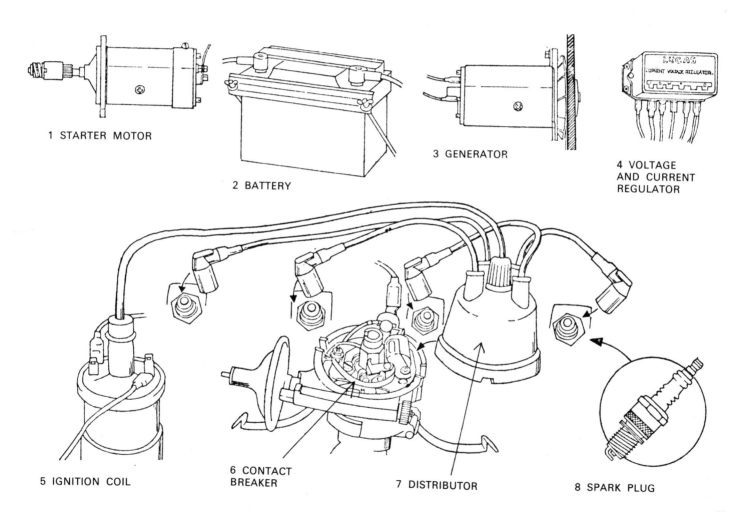

1 STARTER MOTOR

2 BATTERY

3 GENERATOR

4 VOLTAGE AND CURRENT REGULATOR

5 IGNITION COIL

6 CONTACT BREAKER

7 DISTRIBUTOR

8 SPARK PLUG

ENGINE STARTS BUT . . .

STALLS IMMEDIATELY

1 Check that choke is operating (p 51).
2 Check condition of spark plugs (p. 61).
  (p. 52).

STALLS AS IT GETS WARM

1 Check that choke is fully out of operation (p 51).
2 Check idling speed of carburettor (p. 52).
3 Check condition of points (p. 58).

IDLES ROUGHLY WHEN FULLY WARM

1 Check tuning of carburettor (p. 52).
2 Check condition of spark plugs (p. 60).

MISFIRES AND SPLUTTERS

1 Clean and check spark plugs (p. 60).
2 Check ignition leads and all connections (p. 58).
3 Check and clean fuel pump (p. 55).
4 Check no intermittent blockages in the fuel supply system (p. 54).
5 Check no water in fuel (if water in fuel is suspected topping up the tank may help because water sinks to the bottom; later lower part of tank can be drained).
6 Check cleanliness of air filter (p. 55).

MISFIRES AT HIGHER REVS

1 Check contact points (p. 58).
2 Check spark plugs (p. 60).
3 Vacuum in petrol tank: remove filler cap and replace it; if engine then runs smoothly for a short time the problem is a blocked fuel-tank vent (p. 54).
4 Check fuel supply lines and unions for air leaks (p. 54).
5 Check for water in the fuel.
6 Cause probably dirt in the carburettor, which will need a thorough professional clean.

LOSS OF ACCELERATION

1 Is correct octane-rating of fuel in use (p. 50)?
2 Is handbrake partly or fully on?
3 Check choke operation at the carburettor (p. 52).
4 Check throttle linkage from accelerator pedal to carburettor.

5 Check air cleaner (p. 55).
6 Check automatic spark advance of distributor (p. 59).
7 Check spark plugs in good condition (p. 60).
8 Check fuel pump and supply lines (p. 54).

ENGINE RUNS BUT . . .

STOPS SUDDENLY

1 Check for broken contact-breaker spring (p. 58).
2 Check for disconnected battery terminal or electrical wire on coil, distributor, etc (p. 57).
3 Check for broken or frayed ignition wires.

COUGHS AND DIES WITH LITTLE WARNING

1 Check petrol gauge, is the tank empty?
2 If you have a mechanical fuel pump allow engine to cool and try again. Fuel vaporisation, particularly in hot weather, often causes this problem.
3 Give fuel pump a light tap and, if it doesn't work, check connections, then clean filter (p. 55).
4 Detach and blow through fuel lines (p. 54).

MISFIRES, STOPS, THEN STARTS AGAIN

1 Check for loose ignition connections.
2 Check for stuck choke in the carburettor (p. 52).

IGNITION LIGHT COMES ON

1 Check fan-belt (p. 41).
2 Switch off engine and check connections to generator.
3 If cause is not found it is safe to drive on to the next garage or AA/RAC service centre.

BACKFIRES

1 Ignition timing is faulty; refer to handbook.

RACES WHILE GOING UPHILL OR UNDER ACCELERATION

1 Check no free play in the clutch pedal (p. 69), then drive slowly to nearest garage using as little throttle as possible.

ELECTRICS FAIL

1 If all electrics — lights, wipers, horn, interior light, etc — fail at once, check battery terminals (p. 57) and earth-strap to bodywork.
2 If one or two electrical components fail — such as wipers and horn — check for a blown fuse (p. 56).
3 If single lights fail check earth connections and bulbs (p. 62).

THINGS GET A BIT HOT . . .

Stop immediately at the first sign of overheating. If the car does not have a temperature gauge, the first sign is probably wisps of steam emerging from under the bonnet. Switch off and lift the bonnet to ventilate the engine.

1 Check fan-belt (p. 41).
2 Check radiator level (p. 44). If engine is hot remove radiator cap very slowly, and at arm's length, covering it with a cloth to prevent jets of steam from scalding the arms. It is better to let the engine cool down for fifteen minutes before removing the cap. If water level is down, top up when the engine cools. If hot, pour only half a cupful of water at a time.
3 Check for radiator leaks.
4 Look for burst or leaking water hose (p. 45).
5 Check condition of radiator cap's rubber seal.
6 Check that air passages through the radiator are not blocked up with oil-bound dust, leaves and other debris: clear with hose or air-jet.
7 If bubbles rise from the radiator while the engine is running the cylinder-head gasket is leaking: seek professional help.
8 Another check for a blown gasket is to inspect the oil dipstick (p. 42): if it shows traces of water, a greyish deposit, or the oil level is higher than it should be, do not use the engine again until it has been checked by a garage.
9 On a cold morning rapid overheating indicates that parts of the cooling jacket are still frozen. Pour warm water over the radiator pipes and check anti-freeze mixture (p. 44).

IF YOU SMELL . . .

BURNING RUBBER

Stop and switch off immediately as a hose may be fouling the hot exhaust manifold. Otherwise the fault is probably electrical — a wire overheating and melting its insulation. To prevent a fire, disconnect the battery immediately.

PUNGENT ODOUR

1 Clutch slipping (p. 69).
2 Brakes binding (p. 66).
3 Handbrake left partly or fully on.
4 Electrical fire (see above).

PETROL

1 Flooded carburettor (p. 82).
2 Over-filled petrol tank.
3 Leaking fuel lines.
4 If you have just pulled out from a service station check that there is no petrol on your shoes.

HOT, RUBBER-SMELLING STEAM

Switch off and check radiator.

IF YOU HEAR . . .

BUBBLING

(when the engine is switched off)
Suspect over-heating.

FAST CLICKING

Fuel pump (p. 54) may be overworking. Check for leaks in the fuel lines.

SCREECHING WHEN STARTING

Check fan-belt (p. 41), generator and water pump (see car handbook); on a cold morning water pump may be frozen.

CLANKS, THUDS, RATTLES, KNOCKS, CLICKS

Investigate at once, get advice from an AA/RAC patrol if possible or go to a garage. Don't shrug it off and hope for the best, because the noise is not normal and probably indicates that a part is wearing out and likely to break. It could affect the safety of the car.

Never do this

Never stop in the middle of the road—it is dangerous and illegal. If you can't drive a car, push it off the road as far as possible. This broken down car is more than just a danger to itself. Those drivers waiting behind will probably become impatient and try to pass—into the line of oncoming cars.

FUNNY THINGS BEGIN TO HAPPEN . . .

LIGHTS GO DIM

1 Fan-belt getting loose (p. 41).
2 Battery low (evident when engine is idling) (p 30).
3 Excessive load (switch off accessories such as radio, heated rear window).

BRAKES . . .

judder when applied.
Check linings (p. 67).

feel spongy.
Air in the hydraulic system (p. 68).

squeal when applied.
Check linings (p. 67).

pull to one side.
Check tyre pressures (p. 46).
Check brake adjustment (p. 67).

TYPICAL LIGHTING AND BRAKING SYSTEMS

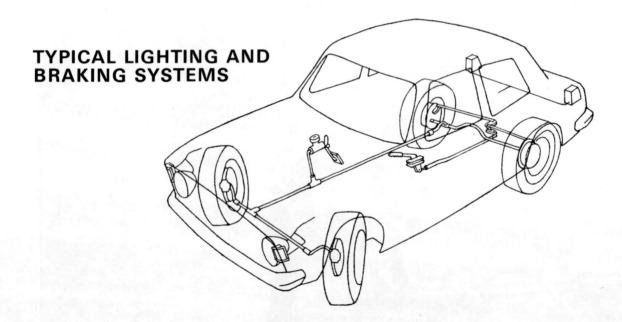

STEERING . . .

wanders from side to side.
Check tyre pressures (p. 46).
Check steering joints for wear (p. 36).
Check suspension for wear (p. 36).

pulls to one side.
Incorrect tyre pressures (p. 46).
Brakes binding on one side (p. 66).
Broken spring (p. 36).

vibrates at certain speeds.
Wheels loose or out of alignment (p. 49).

GEARS . . .

crunch when selecting first gear.
Idling speed too high, adjust carburettor (p. 54).

crunch when changing gears.
Check clutch adjustment and wear (p. 69).

are difficult to change, or stick.
Check clutch adjustment and wear (p. 69).

CAR VIBRATES WHILE COASTING

Check tyres and wheels for bulges or damage (p. 49).

TYPICAL STEERING AND TRANSMISSION LAYOUT

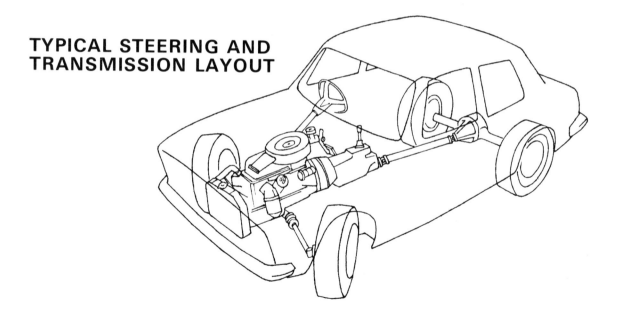

HOW TO GET OUT OF A
JAM IF YOU . . .

LOSE THE IGNITION KEY

1 Disconnect the ignition switch at the coil (this is the terminal on top of the coil marked SW, or the one which has a thin wire which does not lead to the side of the distributor)
2 Identify the earth terminal of the battery. It has a short thick wire strap bolted to the body of the car
3 Connect a thin insulated wire between the battery terminal which is not earthed and the coil terminal marked SW
4 Operate starter by pressing rubber-capped button on the solenoid (see car handbook for exact location).

(NB. If the coil terminals are marked only + and − identify which battery terminal is earthed to the car body, then run a wire from the other battery terminal to the coil terminal which has the same sign.)

LOCK THE KEYS IN THE CAR

Apart from calling in the AA/RAC, the only emergency course of action is to break the side window and reach in for the keys.

Sometimes it is possible to work a thin wire through the window to release the door lock. Or if it is a sliding window it is fairly easy to overcome the latch.

The best answer is prevention rather than cure: wire a spare key underneath the car or keep one in a small magnetic box which can be clipped out of sight to a corner under one of the wings.

CATCH FIRE

1 Stop and switch off immediately.
2 Abandon car.
3 If flames have not yet started disconnect battery.
4 If flames are seen lift bonnet a fraction and fan fire extinguisher from side to side. Throwing open the bonnet and trying to beat out the flames is unlikely to succeed and is dangerous.

SHATTER A WINDSCREEN

1 Avoid jerking the steering wheel or panic-braking.
2 If there is no clear-view zone, with clenched fist and straight arm smartly punch a hole through the glass in front of you to restore vision.
3 Pull into the side and stop.

4 The law requires full forward vision, so all the glass fragments must be removed before driving on. Do not leave glass on the road or verge.
5 When driving without a windscreen wind up all windows and increase speed only until the air pressure inside the car is neutral. This point is often marked by a faint fluttering in the air inside the car. If you try to drive faster the rear window may pop out.
6 Carrying a plastic emergency windscreen is a good idea.

BURST A TYRE

1 Keep a firm hold of the steering wheel and steer a straight course.
2 If the puncture is in a rear tyre pump the brakes firmly and draw into the side.
3 If the trouble is in a front tyre, brake as gently as possible (braking throws the weight of the car on to the affected wheel).
4 Switch on hazard lights as early as possible.

GET STUCK

In mud:

1 Use high gears and low revs, don't skid the wheels.
2 Try rocking the car between reverse and second gear to lift the wheel out of the hole.
3 Lay a track of scrub (bracken, heather, dry grass, hay) in front of each wheel, or lay down sacks, wire netting.

In sand:

1 Keep revs as low as possible, using high gears and taking care not to skid the wheels.
2 Lay down a track of sacks or wire netting.
3 Once you get moving try not to stop.

MEET A FLOOD

1 Test the water for depth: on no account should it reach the fan, which will throw a thick spray over the engine and let water into the carburettor, with dire results.
2 Drive slowly so the 'bow wave' does not flood the engine.
3 Keep revs high so water does not enter the exhaust pipe.
4 Driving through salt water in this fashion is very damaging unless the car is immediately hosed down with fresh water, paying particular attention to the underbody surfaces.
5 Test and dry out brakes before continuing.

HIT HEAVY SNOW OR SNOW DRIFTING ON THE ROAD

1 Slow right down.
2 Keep moving.
3 Use high gears and low revs so wheels do not spin.
4 Do not alter tyre pressures.
5 Fit chains if possible.
6 Brake gently.

EMERGENCY PRECAUTIONS

A driver's first duty is to other motorists. If you break down pull as far off the road as possible. Place a red warning triangle (at night a red flashing torch) at least twenty-five yards behind the car. If the car is stopped on a blind bend where it is a hazard, take every step immediately to warn other traffic.

On a motorway, do not remain on the hard shoulder a moment longer than necessary — it is a dangerous place. Pull as far over to the left as possible — on to the grass if you can. If changing a wheel on the offside have somebody standing near you, to watch oncoming traffic and warn of vehicles wandering on to the hard shoulder. The safest place for car passengers to be is up the bank, well out of the way.

UNDER-THE-BONNET JARGON

GLOSSARY OF SOME COMMON MOTORING TERMS

AXLE-TRAMP   Hopping movement of back wheels which causes the car to lose grip on the road when accelerating or cornering.

BHP (brake horsepower)   Measurement of the actual power of an engine, from its ability to turn a machine called a brake dynamometer.

BRAKE-FADE   Decrease of braking efficiency due to linings becoming overheated; usually occurs during a long descent.

COMPRESSION RATIO   Amount by which the mixture of petrol and air in the cylinder is compressed by the upward movement of the piston before the spark plug ignites it; if the mixture is compressed to one-tenth the compression ratio is said to be 9:1.

DECOKE   Engine maintenance involving the cleaning of carbon deposits from valves, pistons, cylinders and cylinder head.

ENGINE BRAKING   Slowing down the car by changing to a lower gear.

FINAL DRIVE   That part of the transmission system which is between the propeller shaft and the back wheels, i.e. differential and half shafts.

FIRING ORDER   Order in which the different pistons of the engine complete their cycles. The order is mixed to prevent the engine vibrating. Typical order of a six-cylinder engine is 1, 5, 3, 6, 2, 4.

FLAT SPOT   Momentary delay between depressing the accelerator and the engine's response; usually due to a carburettor fault.

FOUR-STROKE   Term used to describe the cycle of each piston in a conventional car. The full cycle is:

1 Sucks petrol and air into cylinder.
2 Moves up and compresses mixture which is fired.
3 Moves down in power stroke that drives the engine.
4 Moves up to expel exhaust gases.

FUEL-INJECTION   System of squirting petrol directly into cylinders as it is needed instead of mixing it in the carburettor.

GASKET   Thin material such as cork, rubber, paper or soft metal which is sandwiched between two metal parts like a washer to make a very tight join.

GEAR RATIO   Relationship between two cogs of different sizes; if the large cog has five times as many teeth as the small one the ratio is 5:1.

GROUND CLEARANCE   Distance between the road and the lowest part of the car (apart from the wheels).

HEEL-AND-TOE   Snappy way of driving using the right foot to control brake and accelerator simultaneously so the car can be changed down a gear to assist braking.

HIGH TENSION (HT)   The high-voltage part of the car's electrical system between the distributor, coil and spark plugs.

HORIZONTALLY OPPOSED   Engine in which cylinders are laid on their sides in such a way that alternate pistons face each other with the crankshaft between them (such as Volkswagen engine).

HORSEPOWER (hp)   Unit of power used to measure the output of the engine.

JET   A tiny opening through which fuel is squirted. A variable jet has a sharp, spring-loaded needle which can be screwed in or out of the hole to vary the size of the opening. Jets are usually found in the carburettor.

KICK-DOWN   Device which enables the driver to over-ride the automatic transmission and obtain a lower gear by sharply depressing the accelerator right to the floor.

KNOCKING   Also known as 'pinking', it is a repeated rapping or thumping noise coming from the engine, usually denoting wear or petrol of too low a grade.

LOW TENSION   Part of the car's electrical system which has a voltage equal to that of the battery (usually 12 volts); it includes practically all electrical circuits except the ignition.

MONOCOQUE (MONO CONSTRUCTION)   Method of carbody construction which relies on a complete shell of pre-stressed metal for strength, rather than a frame bolted on a chasis. Also known as 'unitary construction'.

MOT TEST   Compulsory annual roadworthiness test which must be obtained at certain garages for vehicles more than three years old; strictly speaking the Ministry of Transport is now the Department of the Environment, although the old name is still used.

MULTIGRADE Type of oil which is suitable for a wide range of temperature conditions and saves the need to replace winter oil (thinner) for summer oil (thicker); usually known as 20W/50W.

NEARSIDE Left-hand side of the car as seen from the driving seat looking ahead.

OFFSIDE Right-hand side of the car as seen from the driving seat looking ahead.

OVERSTEER Tendency of the car to turn a corner more sharply than the driver might expect from the angle of the steering wheel.

PINKING See **Knocking.**

PISTON SLAP Tapping noise made by pistons touching the sides of the cylinders; indicates engine wear.

REBORE Overhaul of engine in which the cylinder bores are re-aligned by making them larger, then fitted with larger pistons.

REMOULD Tyre on which all the tread rubber has been renewed; unsuitable for high speeds or high loads.

RETREAD Tyre on which some of the rubber has been renewed and a new tread pattern cut; these tyres are illegal for cars.

REVOLUTION ('REV') One complete turn of the crankshaft of the engine.

REV-COUNTER (TACHOMETER) Instrument for measuring the speed of the engine expressed in revolutions per minute (rpm).

RICH MIXTURE A mixture of petrol and air in which the proportion of petrol exceeds 1 : 15 (the chemically correct mixture of petrol to air).

SAE The Society of Automobile Engineers, an American standards organisation, draws up specifications for such things as oil grades and nut sizes; the initials are used to indicate that the product meets the agreed specification.

SERVO Device to assist the driver to apply force, usually fitted to steering or brakes (power-assisted).

STEERING RATIO Amount the steering wheel has to be turned compared to how far the front wheels of the car actually turn.

STROKE Distance between the upper and lower limits of piston movement in the cylinder.

SUPPRESSOR Device fitted to ignition circuit of car to prevent interference with radio and TV reception in nearby houses.

SYNCHROMESH Gear-box mechanism which automatically adjusts the speed of spinning cogs so they mesh easily and without causing damage.

TACHOMETER See **Rev-counter.**

THOU Abbreviation for one-thousandth of an inch, usually applied to fine clearances such as the distance between spark-plug electrodes, contact-breaker points, etc.

TOE-IN/OUT Expression used to describe relative angles of front wheels. Toe-in describes both wheels pointing inwards; toe-out describes the reverse.

TORQUE The turning force of the engine. (Its ability to turn the crankshaft which turns the transmission and ultimately turns the wheels.)

TRACK Width between the centres of the tracks made by the tyres.

TURNING CIRCLE Circumference of the tightest circle the car can turn with full steering lock applied.

TWO-STROKE Type of engine used mainly for motor-cycles and such things as lawn-mowers in which each piston makes only two strokes (one down and one up) for each cycle of combustion.

UNDERSTEER Tendency of a car to turn less sharply than the steering wheel, so the wheel has to be turned further than the driver would expect.

VETERAN Car made before the end of 1904.

VINTAGE Car made between 1919 and 1930 inclusive.

WEAK MIXTURE Mixture of petrol and air in which the proportion of petrol is lower than 1 : 15 and is therefore less efficient for combustion.

WHEELBASE Distance between the centres of the front and rear wheels.

WHEEL HOP Rapid up and down movement of one of the back wheels.

ORGANISATIONS
THAT CAN HELP

Automobile Association,
Fanum House, Basing View, Basingstoke, Hants RG21 2EA

Institute of Advanced Motorists,
Empire House, Chiswick High Road, London W4 5TJ

Motor Agents' Association,
201 Great Portland Street, London W1N 6AB

Royal Automobile Club,
RAC House, Lansdowne Road, Croydon, Surrey CR9 2JA

Royal Scottish Automobile Club,
Blythswood Square, Glasgow G2 4AG